W9-AEC-064

These Moderns

Some Parisian Close-ups

By
F. RIBADEAU DUMAS

Translated from the French by
FREDERIC WHYTE

With a preface by
DOROTHY RICHARDSON

Illustrations by Pierre Payen

KENNIKAT PRESS
Port Washington, N. Y./London

THESE MODERNS

First published in 1932
Reissued in 1971 by Kennikat Press
Library of Congress Catalog Card No: 71-113308
ISBN 0-8046-1357-5

Manufactured by Taylor Publishing Company   Dallas, Texas

Not so very long ago it was customary to declare that interest in a writer should stop short at his work. Any desire to know more of him was called idle curiosity. The assertion could at least claim noble birth. It originated with first-class critics of first-class work; and the first-class critic is one who knows that artists are mortal and would jealously shelter their privacies from the vulgar gaze, leaving to represent them only the results of their working hours when they are more than themselves. So far so good. And it is probable that most writers at their best, and worst, moments desire not only to remain unknown but to be forever anonymous. For no one knows the name of the power we call inspiration, though many have described it after their manner. And the writer's desire for recognition, save in the case of those who are possessed, as was for example Émile Zola, of the determination to crush by sheer weight every antagonist, to make their school the only school and themselves its head, is the desire to be certain of his own authenticity to know that what means everything to him is no delusion of his own spirit but reaches that of others also. Without this recognition he is left uncertain.

But when recognition took the form of what used to be called "vulgar curiosity," one of two things happened: either he fled, or, if hard pressed,

91769

put up an imposing façade. As did every man. All of us have "two soul-sides, one to face the world with" and one to show to those who love us. Montaigne and Rousseau, it is true, scorned the façade and got home to the world at large by the frankness of their self-revelation; using themselves as material for their art, they reached the self in the reader. Their humane wisdom would lose half its force without the accompanying revelation of personal weakness and inconsistency. And Montaigne and Rousseau were fore-runners. How slight, in face of modern self-revelations, seem even their most intimate confessions. How puzzled would they be, how difficult would they find it to answer some of the problems we could set for them to-day. Puzzled and amazed. For, like our investigation of matter, our analysis of human motives has gone so far that there is now no sure ground for confident assertion. Generalisations abound. The mind-doctors ceaselessly dispute. We know not what we are.

But we know we are stranger even than we thought and the processes of investigation have cured us of shame. Reticence, even in England, is no longer an undisputed virtue. Modern psychology, in shifting the centre of human interest from the world about us—now, as to its surface, fully explored—to mankind, even to the innermost recesses of the human spirit, has joined forces with art, to whose power of revealing these recesses it pays full tribute.

Perhaps the most significant feature of the old attitude towards man's interest in the personality and *vie intime* of those who make his books, is that while it was deprecated on behalf of living writers, the moment the artist was in his coffin, or at least the moment his immediate descendants were in theirs, it was encouraged in every possible way. There is a perpetual searching. Any documentary evidence, any shred of detail, the homelier the better, bearing on the salient dead, is more and ever more eagerly welcomed. Imagine the hullabaloo that would go up if suddenly someone discovered Homer's diary.

This eagerness with regard to the past flatly contradicts the dogma of the sufficiency of a man's work and the irrelevance of personalia. If a posthumous nude exposure is valuable, so also is a current nude exposure. We were shy of it. To some extent we still are. It has been well said that a study of a modern nude, if dated B.C., will pass muster anywhere, but if the same study be labelled "Portrait of Mrs. X.", society would stampede.

But though intimate knowledge of a writer's way of life may be essential to a just appreciation of his work, it is nevertheless secondary to that work and it were better we should meet him first in his achievements. Far better to go straight to books and form our own opinions of them, and of their authors, than first to read of the books and their authors and then to seek them out. But our modern world grants this course in its purity to very few. Books are innumerable. We must perforce select. And most of us depend for our selection upon the reports of friends or of the accredited astronomers of the literary firmament. And unless we are of those strange beings who, when a new book is mooted, turn immediately to an old one (forgetting that this once was brand new, and, since it has survived, something worse: "new-fangled," their pet abomination), we like to be told when a new star comes into sight.

But though it is best to read as far as possible without prejudice, with the minimum of foreknowledge, in a word, with our own eyes, to know first the work and only afterwards to learn by reading or enquiry something of the author and his standing, at the same time it is better to read about authors and their books and then to read the books than not to read at all. And in the case of foreign authors, new authors not so far translated, for the large majority of us there is nothing for it but to read about them and hope for translation. Even for the linguist, and where translations are to hand, foreign authors are usually preceded by heralds. And when, on behalf of the group of young men and young women now working in Paris, the herald happens to be Monsieur F. Ribadeau Dumas, who has met and talked with them all and vividly set down his thoughts and impressions, we have an introduction to contemporary French writers that leaves us with the impression of having ourselves visited them, and we may be grateful to Mr. Frederic Whyte for attempting the impossible: the putting into English of this ultra-Parisian *causerie*. Dramatic always, at once sympathetic and intelligent, certain of the author's allusions and turns of phrase and thought are unintelligible save to those who know their Paris through and through in its fresh developments. But the necessary omissions, for those who wish to know something of the lives and ideas of young France as represented by writers who have already made or are in process of making their mark, are negligible. Those who read without much preliminary knowledge enter a fresh field of interest. Those who have already read themselves into acquaintance with the authors here depicted will be pleased to meet them in their homes.

Artists, life's irregulars, vary from race to race. There is in the French a re-assuring consistency. The French author would seem to live more "artistically" than do most Britons of the same persuasion. And it is not quite that he desires to do so, deliberately dramatises his life. It is a fundamental difference of tone. That is the essence of nationality and the zest of international exchanges.

DOROTHY RICHARDSON.

Without actually attempting a translation of the book, no one can guess the difficulty of turning into intelligible and idiomatic English these sprightly but elliptical pen-portraits. Here and there—notably on pp. 62, 136, 139, 165-8—I have called in the help of a more accomplished and more daring hand: I say "more daring," because the few passages in question take greater liberties with the original than I have ventured upon. If I myself have anywhere been over-bold it has been in the freedom with which, throughout the volume, I have omitted words and phrases that I felt would merely puzzle the English reader.

FREDERIC WHYTE.

CONTENTS

CONTENTS

I
PRINCES OF THE PEN

PIERRE BENOIT

PIERRE BENOIT

We were dining with a member of the Academy. Pierre Benoit and a bishop had been exchanging riddles. The ruby hue of the wine lent warmth to Monseigneur's amethyst ring. Henry Bordeaux told of his recent visit to Mussolini. Benoit, now already grown a legendary figure, declaimed some splendid lines. "Who wrote them?" he asked. We all vied in our panegyrics on them, given out so effectively in the deep tones of the great novelist, himself a poet too. Some guessed them to be by Maurice Rostand, some by Henri de Régnier. "Boileau!" And while we all laughed over our display of ignorance, Benoit went on to declare that he was constantly using in his own stories classic phrases which no one ever recognized. We pressed him for instances, but instead of giving us any he recited for us his famous pastiche on Madame Anna de Noailles. . .

A Prince of the Pen, alike by his world-wide vogue and by the perfection of his craftsmanship. Pierre Benoit is Olympian in his outward aspect. There is something about him of the Roman consul, with his heavy jowl and the thick neck buried in the big shoulders. His bass voice is strong and resonant. Normally solemn, almost with a tragic air, his face will suddenly brighten into the sunniest radiance. He is the wittiest and least pretentious of men. You are won to him in a moment by his naturalness and his humour. His

memory of books is inexhaustible. Racine and
Victor Hugo are his favourite authors . . . Public
affairs have claimed him for a moment—he was a
member of the ministerial staff of Léon Bérard.
"How I would have liked to go in for politics!" he
once confessed to me, "but that was impossible."

The newspapers are always inventing new
fables about him. They will tell you how he is
buried in the Île aux Oiseaux and working away
in solitude. In reality, as likely as not, the new
book in question—"Erromango," perhaps—will
have come into existence at Versailles, amidst a
setting of flower vases and sparkling fountains.
Benoit would have borne himself with elegance
in the Versailles minuets of old.

His extraordinarily acute powers of observation, his well-stored mind and his gift of fancy
and invention lend wealth to his copious talk no
less than to his writings. These attributes were
accountable for the immediate triumph of
"l'Atlantide" and of the ten novels which followed, and have made him the foremost storyteller of our time. Like a practised linotypist,
Benoit lets his hands travel over the keyboard,
producing at will those works which call forth our
curiosity and delight and leave us dreaming. He
possesses the philosopher's stone which tells him
he secret of his reader's sensibilities. His methods
recall sometimes those of a clock-maker, some-

times those of a motor-engineer. He is an incomparable mechanician, contriving for us with incredible facility now the mirages of the desert, now treasures of some palace of enchantment, now the fascinating imbroglio of a love drama. Exotic scenes, marvels of luxury, lend their fascination to his tales. Astounding adventures to which he manages to give an atmosphere of reality, mysteries of a dream-like, rose-hued Orient in which barbarous young queens exercise their fatal seductions—these are the things he excels in, tales full of wonder, yet told with touches of that mocking scepticism so dear to him.

He has confessed that he sets about writing books in just the way in which as a boy he set to work doing a lesson at school. He deserves full marks for the results. The technique he has attained is perfect. He has achieved a method which could not be bettered.

Boldly, fearlessly, but with a certain air of ingenuousness, he enters into the very heart of the historical theme which he has chosen. We are wont when talking of his "Koenigsmark," his "Pour Don Carlos," his "La Chaussée des Géants" as historical novels, to compare them with those of Alexandre Dumas. Benoit, however, has recourse to history only for the element of credibility which it lends him for his purposes. Our interest is evoked unfailingly when some historical event is enacted before our eyes, when something that really happened is in question. A story based upon recorded fact has a stronger hold on one. The types of Frenchmen taking part in the action are all familiar to us: army officers, state officials, representatives of the average everyday France of the Third Republic . . .

No kind of story is so machine-made and so impersonal in appearance. Yet in them the author reveals himself to us completely. His wealth of irony—which amounts almost to mockery when he is dealing with Gambetta—his enjoyment of his task, his alertness of mind, his relish for decoration and ornamentation, his gusto for history, his essential bourgeois Frenchness, so racy of our soil—all point unmistakably to Pierre Benoit, *gascon et fonctionnaire*. "I was born at Albi, my father lives at Dax; Gascony and the Basque country are my home-land." His stories often have for their background the Landes, those Landes of "Mademoiselle de la Ferté," which produce a certain wine—*vin des sables* as it is described—for which he would seem to have a liking. It is from the causticity and the verve of the South that he gets his gift of humour, so guileless to all appearance although at times so devastating. His whole temperament, his very appetite, even his *embonpoint*, are all of the Midi. The shrewd intelligence of the Pyrenæan peoples accounts for his political leanings, while implanting in him at the same time his love of the soil.

If his university training initiated him into the delights of learning, the Sorbonne opened out to him the treasures of French literature. Thus was laid the groundwork of his love for the past. Talking of the researches which he made while engaged in thinking out his "Koenigsmark," he said to me: "Flaubert once planned to write a Koenigsmark, but he was deterred by the labour involved . . . What a tremendous amount of labour it did involve! But I realized how boring all the documentation would be to my readers, so I spared them and distilled my documents into a romance. That was how I worked also in 'l'Atlantide.' "

For a period he was curator of the Library of Public Instruction, and while occupying this post he had ample opportunity for his historical delvings. Even to-day he never writes a novel without six or eight months of preliminary research.

To his study of history he owes much: the growth of his mind, no less than the themes of his books—Carlist wars, Irish revolts, Syrian episodes, Prussian episodes . . . He is a psychologist no less than an historian. This is to be noted especially in "Mademoiselle de la Ferté" and in "Axelle," with their analysis of the *comédie humaine*. "I am always re-reading Balzac," Benoit once said to me.

Master of himself no less than of his art, never employing his immense gifts otherwise than deliberately, has Benoit enslaved himself overmuch to the too rigorous system which he has adopted? He himself feels so. The writer who set out to win the great public and who has succeeded in doing so to such an astonishing degree is unable now to desert the colours of Success! "I write for the average Frenchman," he confesses.

Barrès gave him his friendship. Paul Bourget has commended him. Henry Bordeaux has sung his praises. Léon Daudet by his glorification of him disturbed the last years of Marcel Proust . . .

Irony is Benoit's outstanding characteristic. How he enjoys his life and his work. What literary capers he cuts! The names of all his heroines from Antinéa to Axelle begin with an A—the outcome of a bet . . . What pranks he has to answer for—anachronisms, deliberate plagiarisms, puzzles, pitfalls, tomfooleries! . . .

HENRI BÉRAUD

HENRI BÉRAUD

When he is not at Saint-Clement-des-Baleines, in an inaccessible retreat on the Île de Ré, and when he is not on one of his journalistic jaunts over Europe, he may perhaps be found in his regular home, but you will have to wait until the middle of the night before climbing up to that studio-dwelling of his in the huge house in the Rue Rochechouart, the steep thoroughfare up and down which the people of Montmartre have to travel by autobus and clattering tramway.

Henri Béraud is impetuous and combative. He has the build of a wrestler and he is overflowing with life. He does as the spirit moves him. And as he is conscious of possessing the energy required for the defence of his ideas, he gives himself his head—that massive, square, hard head of his. He is capable of strangling a rascal with one hand while with the other he lavishes alms upon someone in need. *"Je ne dépends de personne"*—"I am dependent upon no one"—is his motto.

He gets up when most people are going to bed and goes to bed when most people are getting up. An uncomfortable existence? No, an existence to his taste. The journalist has knocked about the world too much, the writer is too solicitous for his freedom, to adapt himself to conventional habits.

A man of ample girth, his waistcoat has a job of it to hold him in. Whether you see him taking down a pipe from the rack within his reach, or adjusting his monocle, or striding up and down his study, lined with books and pictures, the while he holds forth to you, he recalls one of those Balzac types that Danton used to love to caricature in little plaster figures and that Daumier immortalized with his pen.

He looks like a member of the Convention, full-blooded, rough, with a mane of black hair already growing grey thrown back from his low forehead. His slightly prominent eyes are notable for their boldness and vivacity. There is a boyishness about him. His *batik* tie shows up from a blue shirt. He wears a decoration. On one extremely white hand is to be seen a ring bearing an Egyptian stone. His utterance, easy, vigorous, often spiced with *gauloiseries*, flows through expressive lips without moving a muscle in any other part of his face. He lowers his head as though about to charge at you. You are reminded that this is the violent pamphleteer of the Léon Daudet type who has dealt such mighty blows at sundry adversaries. His energy is inexhaustible. He is all life and ardour and go: the arch-type of the militant pressman. "Capable of everything," he says himself, "except low tricks and making my fortune." He has worked for almost every newspaper and review and has many books to his credit.

He has made some famous journeys. He was one of the earliest explorers of Soviet Russia; he

has described post-war Germany, Ireland in
rebellion, Greece in turmoil. He has interviewed
the great men of the world. He has collected some
of the best pages in his "Flâneur Salarié." Meanwhile he has exercised his talents as a writer of
books in "Le Vitriol de Lune," "Lazare" and "Au
Capucin Gourmand" . . . An artist and a dreamer,
fascinated by life, his love of history is in keeping.
I have always possessed the taste for history," he
tells me. "I obtain an intense vision of certain
scenes and I feel the historical thrill—it is in my
nature." He has written "Le Bois du Templier
Pendu," "Le Second Amour du Chevalier des
Grieux," and "Mon Ami Robespierre" . . . "I
have tried to reproduce the atmospheres," he
says.

A majestic tea-kettle is a-boil on the studio
stove. Talleyrand, Boileau, Régnard, Racine
and Gluck preside over our talk, looking down on
us from their pedestals. On one wall hangs a proclamation of the year 1803. Some valuable books
lie about, keeping company with fifteen hundred
phonograph records.

The key to this man's strong personality, solid,
French, often Rabelaisian, at the same time sentimental, full of delicate feeling, disposed to
mockery and ever ready for a fight? We shall find
it in his life.

"I am a Lyonnais and a Wagnerian," he will

29

tell you. He is the son of a baker who practised his trade beneath the sign of *La Gerbe d'Or*. In the outlying regions of Lyons he spent his boyhood, going to school and playing truant, always laughing, always up to tricks, looking on at the drama of life in the streets, and already very easily roused. His memories of those days may be read in his little book, "La Gerbe d'Or," a record of deep feelings blended of sweetness and sadness, for a sensitive heart is always melancholy, never at rest.

After school, the lycée, the usual legal studies, followed by work as an antiquary's assistant, as a wine-merchant's assistant, as an actor and as a singer—for he had developed a baritone voice. Then work at a bookseller's, in an insurance agency, and in a workshop where designs for silk embroideries were made. Then the war. While serving as an artillery officer at the front he met Gustave Téry, to whom he owes his great career as a journalist, for it was Téry who prevented him from returning to Lyons and continuing his hundred and one occupations there.

The baker's boy of Lyons was soon a famous writer. For several years he acted as dramatic critic for the *Mercure de France*; he has been also the literary editor of a daily paper; to-day he is wedded to his pen. "But don't forget," he declares "that I am a skilled artisan!"

He has no needs; he disregards politics and has no taste for racing. After seven years of journalistic conflict and forty years of the battle of life, he has won repose. He is able to devote himself to his favourite enjoyment, literature, and, while remaining the fighting controversialist, the pamphleteer full of fire, he shuts himself up with his books and his memories, for he has had a surfeit of life. His hair is prematurely touched with grey. Like those seafaring folk who set one thinking of wide horizons, his eyes reflect the most opposite extremes of human nature.

Everywhere he has come up against the drama of life, having had to live.

We shall not soon forget that literary adventure of his, "1930," which called forth so much commotion a couple of years ago. In it he saluted the younger generation and exclaimed: "We are a dawn!" These words should be set beside those of Francis Carco and of Roland Dorgelès . . . and beside the words of all those who took part in the war and who, after it was over, felt suddenly that they had grown old. "And never has the world known so swift a change. . ."

FRANCIS CARCO

FRANCIS CARCO

Friendly, gentle Carco, fresh from writing one of his books, his mouth still full of wickednesses. The wavy lock of hair smoothed down over one eye draws you to him. A versifier, with florid cheeks, fleshy nose and rounded chin. His upper lip lifts as he banters you, disclosing a ravaged set of teeth. The rounded outlines of his clumsy body, his plump hands, his pearl-grey trousers and red shoes, proclaim aloud that he is a Bohemian and with a heart. No neck. A tie of draught-board pattern. An alert, clairvoyant, *gamin*-like look about him. He keeps company with a collection of scapegraces of his own sort. If M. Paul Bourget has handed over to him his analytical tools, Villon the bandit has bequeathed him his lyre.

The rue de Douai climbs up the side of the Butte. A gunshot away from the Moulin Rouge, a few yards away from the Place Blanche and the Place Pigalle, "Franco," as his friends call him, opens his window blinds upon the *milieu* of his diversions and of his inventions. At night the eyes of this region, red eyes, blue eyes, green eyes, take fire and begin to glitter. The pavements become populous. The gas-jets pale. There are clashes of jazz. It is the hour for the *petit verre*. Jésus-la-Caille, Verotchka and la Fernande have appeared at the café at the corner. The night has begun. Some joy, some vice, much misery, at the feet of the great white tutelary cathedral.

Where else could I pay Carco a visit?

Montmartre is his quarter, his home. Montmartre and he are the same thing. The walls of his room are covered with pictures. Here is one of the Moulin, here one of a deserted street, both signed by Utrillo. Here is a spongy production of de Segonzac's, a bather. Derain, Daragnès are both represented. There are some pictures by Suzanne Valadon, some crayon sketches by Luc Albert Moreau: young women behind a bar, dubious-looking folk, two men embracing. Some pictures of nude women by Pascin in his vaporous style. A wooden statuette of the Virgin turns aside from one of a prostitute. A nude figure of a girl by Modigliani, a tender, frank production, seems to blush. There is a phonograph. Blue rugs, nailed down. "I was the first to discover the painters," Carco declares.

Carco has just returned from Spain. Following Théophile Gautier and Barrès, Henry de Montherlant and Jacques de Lacretelle, and so many others, Carco has seen Spain; he has explored all its hovels. He had most entertaining things to tell me. "This journey will have a great influence over me," he added, "and over my way of composing a novel." And his mouth twisted. His face seemed all lip. There was a hunter's look in his eye. You could picture him at work, his hat down over his nose, just as Dignimont has drawn him.

He clipped his words short, left out half his sentences, coined new bits of slang every second.

A dozen books—fiction, volumes of essays and of memories. He is forty-two. Having become an "expert" in the alarming world of law-breakers and notably in that of *messieurs les apaches*, his books are renowned and his heroes have become legendary. The French Academy has conferred on him the *Grand Prix du Roman*.

"I have so keen a taste, so constant a taste, for the street," he says, "that it puts everything else in the shade and make me neglect other things." It was not mere curiosity, therefore, that led him into *bals-musette* and kept him tramping about cities all night long. Ever since his birth at Nouméa he has tramped about over France from frontier to frontier and from one town to another. He goes wherever his fancy may take him. A schoolmaster called him in his youth "the herald of vice." His best years as a young poet were spent in the company of the wild young Bohemians whom he has pourtrayed in "De Montmartre au Quartier Latin." It was a heroic age in that world of painters and poets who had for their masters Picasso and Max Jacob: Shall we ever know how much our literature owes to Max Jacob and the rue Ravignan? Jean de Tinan advised him to study the lowest types of prostitutes and he did so. The habitué of the *Lapin*

Agile and the *Belle Gabrielle* made his way down to the canal Saint-Martin, where the slaughter houses are. The terrible little *voyous* fascinated him. It was then he began to make acquaintance with that *élite* of the Paris world of crime in which he was to specialise with such success. And we may compare with some of Dostoievsky's writings those sections of his books wherein dreadful human wrecks glide beneath lowering skies along sombre and sinister byways. *Romans de mœurs* they are, objective, mordant, bitter: "To run Truth to earth, to discover Truth, to pourtray Truth's features—to have no other love"—in some such words Carco defines his purpose.

He has been condemned for his choice of prostitutes and pimps as a subject, and he grew anxious to free himself from this reproach. Perhaps he even went so far as to disown those first novels which made his fame. Yielding to the persuasions of Paul Bourget, he wrote "Verotchka l'Etrangère," dedicated to Maurice Barrès and depicting ruined princesses; then "Rien qu'une Femme," a psychological novel pure and simple. But he returned to his *milieu*; "L'Amour Vénal" enables one to see how well he knows that *milieu*. And why should he resist his own inclinations?

" 'La Rue,' on which I am busy," he told me, "is a study of this human chaos—a more profound study than I dared to hope." Carco had no need to plan out his return to the theme; the return effected itself. Since the time when he wrote "Jésus-la-Caille" he had gone deeper and deeper in his knowledge of man as he reveals himself when his instincts are let loose. From picturesque presentation of the malefactor, Carco went on to an analysis of the soul. The primitive being under study, whether Bouve or the Milord, suggested endless investigations while revealing the tangled web of his conscience and of his impulses. What else was it but a revival of his old methods when, while keeping within the "fete of Montmartre," he began to choose for his subjects assassins, the prostitutes of the Rue Pigalle, the young provincial, the votary of cocaine, recounting his memories, writing essays full of individuality and originality, disclosing as he did in a paper on *art averti* (which will assuredly live) the "Légende de la Vie d'Utrillo"? In the particular examples of this social scum, in these dregs of the populace to which his enquiry and chance confined him, he touched with his finger the heart of humanity, its rebellions and its despairs, in short the secret torment of all classes, whose tragedy becomes so visible when the individual is thrown into the street. That assassin in his cap— what a wonderful specimen he was, with his violence, his dangerous animal rages, his *climat*, as

Maurois would say! . . . And all these crimes and revelries, do they not help to explain the pangs and terrors of the post-war period?

The nostalgia of exile is known to him. "When the night falls, you see, I feel an irresistible yearning to wander through the streets, and lose myself in them, irrationally, to hear my heart beat beneath the bitterness of the nocturnal scenes one comes upon." This same *dépaysement* forces him to leave for abroad in order to write his books; in a few days' time he will be off to Antwerp to compose "La Rue" . . .

ROLAND DORGELÈS

ROLAND DORGELÈS

They don't make up a team, but the same hand fashioned the lot of them. Their books appeared together on the day when Peace was declared and Fortune emptied out her horn of abundance over them. Pierre Benoit, Henri Béraud, Francis Carco and Dorgelès: a Montmartre battalion, a fighting battalion, all of them, the older and younger men alike, consecrated Princes of the Pen.

Dorgelès made his début as a farceur. Amongst the innumerable stories told of him, that of Boranali, the ass, is the most memorable. Tomfoolery of a wholesome simple kind has always been his *forte.**

Emilie Charmy, that taciturn Lyonnaise who has captured in her portraits the secret of certain souls, has revealed the inner melancholy of this lively man in a painting so vivid that it is like an hallucination. His hair falls down over his face from his too massive forehead. His eyes, with their dark lashes, have a faraway look in them; they seem about to weep, they give the lie to the caustic lips. A mobile, contradictory face. A whimsical fellow. "*Gascon honoraire*," he calls himself—he was

---

*An ass to whose tail he tied a brush with which, while he patiently fed it, it swished on to a large canvas "an impressionist composition!" This he entitled "Sunset on the Adriatic" and exhibited at the gallery of the Independents. It was greeted, as he hoped, by some critics as the "most original and revolutionary" picture of the year.—*Translator*.

born at Amiens. "I am a *cigale* blown too far north by the Mistral" . . . A strong head, an inflammable heart. A true instinct, words to make you laugh, eagerness to persuade you. Quick gesticulations.

Heaping up a pile of cushions, he settles himself on the divan and puts his feet on a small table, relishing his idleness.

He stresses all his words, emphasizes them, draws them out. In his knitted grey overall he looks like an artist. "Painting is the best of all professions," he declares. "All painters sing while they work." Swiftly he outlines an idea, demolishes a prejudice, sets one's thoughts moving, sends forth a batch of picturesque words. His plan of existence is all cut and dried. His independence is that of a fighter, of a French boxer, who knows himself a master of the *savate*.

For a number of years he was a journalist, a writer of paragraphs, a reporter, a gossip . . . The War? "Just a melting pot for humanity," he says. "That is how writers are made." He goes straight ahead, watches, listens, learns, hoping that his curiosity may never be satiated, that his mind will continue filming for ever. Everything intrigues him, astonishes him, excites him. Few are the days he spends in this crowded little flat of his, with its colour scheme of *rose fondant*, yellow and plum.

Raising his eyes, Dorgelès draws my attention to the portrait of Aristide Bruand by Toulouse Lautrec, hung above his writing table. The famous singer, wearing his monumental cape, is shown in profile beneath his immense wide-brimmed felt hat, and with his loose red muffler round his chin and neck . . . Following in the footsteps of Carco and Mac Orlan, Dorgelès thinks of recording his memories of Montmartre.

In a corner of the room is a photograph, very dark and not noticeable at first; it shows a cross, seen by night—that of Thiaumont; and, beneath a little holy water font: "That is a rosary I picked up in the ruins of the church of Neuville-Saint-Vaast." We are suddenly back in the War. "Toute la guerre, avec ses chants et ses sanglots," Dorgelès has written somewhere.

The wild gang of Montmartre artists and poets were among the first to make their way into the trenches; the cadets came later. The older men hold together as the War Generation, "branded with a terrible stamp." They will never forget the War; it may be found in all their books. Their dead comrades are still with them. Dorgelès is the author of "Croix de Bois," a book written in flashes. Only the other day, when the tenth anniversary of the Armistice was being celebrated, and his brain was congested with memorable dates and the long procession of those gone, he exclaimed: "I want to get rid of all these horrors and to be free of them and to herald the promised Peace and the Renascence of the Earth. But no, I cannot . . . I see them marching along before my eyes. . . ."

This feeling of fraternity with the dead permeates dark hours and bright hours alike—the latter animated by memories of the *poilus* in their merry moments and of all the joys of the soldiers' life in common. Roland Dorgelès is the true French fighting man by reason of his blithe spirit. He is the only real War writer, the most truthful and the most beguiling; he has immortalized the resourceful infantry man . . . The friendly slaps, the jovial horseplay, the moments of pride and audacity. The pre-eminence of the bold and laughing French fighting man, sensitive in the extreme, is to be found in "Croix de Bois" and in "Cabaret de la Belle Femme." Duhamel has exalted the sufferings of the martyrs to duty; Barbusse has described the horrors; Dorgelès has glorified the comradeship. The French journalist has proved himself an incomparable observer. The names of Zola and Erckmann-Chatrian come often back to the mind when one talks of Dorgelès . . .

Seated on the divan, I stroke a lion's skin *à la Tartarin*. A glass globe with a map of the world on it shines forth beside me. A head of Angkor in stone wears an unchanging smile. A silver-handled Bedouin knife is stained with the blood of captives. An Indian idol preaches serenity. "I can do only two things—write and travel!" Dorgelès says . . .

Pictures and sketches of travel, descriptions of things seen, raillery and sentiment—of such is his literary domain. Why encumber himself with documentation, why weigh himself down with prejudices and anxieties? The author of "La Caravane sans Chameaux" believes in being himself and no one else; and, selecting with art from all the captivating cries of the entire globe, he witnesses to the lyrical character of his epoch; observation comes once more to its own, to the place usurped by psychological analysis. . .

Boldly he climbs the pyramids: "C'est affreux!" A new kind of crusader, believing but questioning, he inspects the Holy Sepulchre and delights in its atmosphere of militancy and quarrelsomeness. He immerses himself in the multicoloured populace. What things he notes and discovers! He presents them to us just as they come . . . Suddenly he pulls himself up. A thought has moved him suddenly. He turns in derision upon the latest Frenchman encountered "doing" Syria in a black alpaca jacket.

He spares nobody. He blames one, criticizes the other. Meet him anywhere on the Boulevards, outside a café; he will condemn the Government, hold forth against religion, tear the army to pieces. While he is talking, a drum begins to beat; a regiment is passing, knapsacks on backs, drums beating, trumpets blowing. Dorgelès stands up, his eye with a haggard look in it . . . "*Ils sont épatants, ces gars-là . . !*" he cries . . . Someone starts the *Marseillaise*. Dorgelès falls into step. He heads the crowd.

GEORGES DUHAMEL

GEORGES DUHAMEL

A plain door, a modest staircase in a studious quarter of Paris. The quarter of the Pantheon and its quiet neighbouring streets in which the great schools and laboratories lie hidden. A diminutive flat. For a moment I almost think it is Salavin, that "big, bespectacled, close-shaven fellow in his chestnut-coloured overcoat," who is expressing so much kind feeling in a handclasp.

An astonishing person to look at. The countenance of a French primitive as Jean Fouquet knew how to paint the type—round-bodied monks made for the contemplative life. A look of humility behind his spectacles, but a look of curiosity, also, amounting almost to penetration. An observant eye of the kind that controls the white hand of the *savant* or the fingers of a surgeon. The stiff, turned-down collar and spotless shirt-cuffs have a medical flavour about them. He speaks without moving his slit-like mouth. . . . "I have given up medicine, so as to devote myself entirely to letters," he explains. "But that first calling of mine pursues me always. I judge like a doctor, I auscultate. All I can do is to diagnose and prognose and prescribe. That is what I have done, for instance, for Russia. Very few people have understood this." . . . In respect to Soviet Russia, in point of fact, Duhamel, after his famous journey to Moscow, advised Europe to adopt an attitude of "armed expectation" or of alert preparedness for action.

This hygienic tendency is observable in Duhamel's home as in his outward bearing. His bookshelves are neatly arranged, the gilt on the bindings is kept polished. Michelet, Plutarch and Buffon stand designedly close together. Georges Duhamel is at pains to have his work and his life in keeping.

"Each one of my books marks a progression, a study; and my real biography, my most profound biography, is it not the story of my thought, as revealed throughout my work? It is the same thing with my journeys. I began by learning to know Europe, then the Mediterranean basin. Now I seek out foreign and distant countries. I make a fresh journey every year and I am still keeping up my medical and surgical practice in so doing. I never mix in politics." . . .

There is in Duhamel no kind of blindness, despite his inexhaustible confidence in what he calls "the reign of the heart." A soberly worked out analysis, the delicate touch of one who dresses a wound, the abnegation of a hospital attendant.

This explains the favour in which he stands with a public growing daily more vast—no longer European merely, but international; for his appeal is universal and all mankind benefits by his researches.

"No politics! But the writer's profession must rise in status and must have a beneficent effect upon the world in which so many sufferings continue unceasingly." This conception, so noble for a writer, testifies to an inner flame and to his ideal: "the redemption of the unhappy world."

Duhamel's whole existence is a corroboration of this. Trace, from his boyhood onwards, the career of this grandson of a peasant, this son of a chemist who succeeded by strenuous efforts in rising in the world by dint of study: an herbalist first, then chemist, then doctor and *savant*. "I am the seventh of eight children and I have changed my domicile forty times." Material poverty of boyhood's days, emotional wealth of a youth in torment; the delicate boy of twelve was already writing his first poems. Medical studies, difficult years during which he followed a variety of callings, even that of correspondence clerk in a lawyer's office.

Then came the founding of "l'Abbaye," in conjunction with Jules Romains, Vildrac and Arcos, impelled by the ideal: "To live like Monks!" But that fantastic retreat, consecrated to poetry and study, could not last. Life reasserted its rights. Suddenly the War broke out—"the horrible adventure." Duhamel was one of those who went through most of its ordeals: fifty months as head of a surgical corps; four thousand surgical cases; two thousand three hundred operations. Thoughts of all this recur in each one of his books: "I have not yet finished with my memories of the War" he says. "Every year I write a new chapter." Sequels to his masterpiece: "Le Vie des Martyrs."

Shall we point to the exquisite poetry of "Le Voyageur" and of "Elégies" . . . to the humanity and sympathy of "Civilisation" and "Confession de Minuit" . . . to the realistic painting, the charming blend in him of emotion and sentiment, or to the wealth of ideas in his plays? Shall we emphasise the poet, or the storyteller, or the musician, or the dilettante artist, so delicate in his touch, or the brother, or the husband, or the friend? We prefer among his writings those that are inspired by a sensitive distress because they treat of the soul: the three "Salavins," "Pierre d'Horeb" and "Les Hommes Abandonnés" . . . Products of the metaphysical anguish that devours him—the anguish of great minds.

"We are the guard in the night. We need lights illuminating the road for at least a hundred yards ahead, in order to see where we are going; and it is already such a problem to know what we are!"

He leans forward over the polished surface of the table and tries to make out his reflection . . .

Perhaps it is Duhamel's weakness that he believes in vivisection, that he places his trust in medical investigation, in anatomical investigation above all. He comes up continually against the unconscious, against the mystery of what is beyond. He would fain always solve it with the confidence of the surgeon. "Salavin," "La Nuit d'Orage," are documents, we feel, which lead infallibly to that mask of Pascal which hangs in his library; by dint of reflecting upon the infinite (and unlike François Mauriac) his steps lead him to religion and to the most definitive type. That is how he pensively carries us along with him on the road he follows.

Duhamel is one of those souls of whom Sainte-Beuve said that they are "so to speak, born Christian," souls who "have need of pity, who went to confession early and who will need to go to confession always . . . and with a despairing humility."

JEAN GIRAUDOUX

JEAN GIRAUDOUX

Was it Gabrielle or Suzanne or Églantine—one or other of the charming young girls who moved their necks so gracefully and all whose gestures were so suave—that introduced me to the diplomatist?

The hall porter dozed upon his leather-covered bench, unconscious of the rattling of the steel chain by which it was attached to the Ministry and which was being blown about a little by the breeze that came in at the window. A number of visitors were waiting to be received in audience. The administrative routine was in progress and I recalled those famous lines from "Bella." Indignant glances followed me; I was the first to enter the room of the novelist and I had arrived last.

Behind a Louis XV table, between the austere lamp and the telephone, sat a grey-hued figure, somewhat fragile in build but with an air of assurance about him. He wore a straw-coloured tie. His clean-shaven face looked rosy and fresh. The mouth was compressed, the lips colourless, the brow prominent, the hair brushed straight back. From behind the defences of tortoise-shell spectacles—the famous *lunettes roses*—two deep-set eyes, blue as the sea, took your measure benevolently.

Jean Giraudoux, the Limousin, brings to the literary Pleiad his elegant smile. And it would seem that all the persons and all the objects surrounding him enjoy the harmony radiating from the kindliness of his voice, cordial, with a hint of reserve in it, from his face "tender and grave" (words he is fond of), and the friendliness that is the mark of his work.

Simplicity, elegance, British reserve. No stress on the "career," no university pedantry, no author's vanity. A refined man of the world, who creates sympathy. In an odour of English soap, and a freshness of health due to sport, which reduces his forty-five years to a seeming thirty . . .

"But the process of government is really a very interesting thing. If it be carried on slowly, so much the more wisely; what is done quickly is always done ill." Perfect optimism of the head of a department, flooded with work, overwhelmed with telephone calls, solicited on all sides, finding bustle "perfectly natural" and our epoch "a magnificent epoch."

In his own home, a quiet provincial house on the *rive gauche*, sitting in a room hung with pictures of great beauty, beside a modern lamp of translucent glass and a stylish cabinet on which lies a Baedeker's Germany, your eyes are drawn towards the verdure of a garden. In an adjoining room portmanteaux are visible, ready strapped.

A Meridional by birth, reverent of traditions by reason of his Latin origin and his education at the École Normale, he could bring to an end his journeys from the Quai d'Orsay only on the same left bank of the Seine and in the heart of Paris, the rue du Pré-au-Clercs. A venerable house with a massive doorway. Its arch is adorned with sculptured figures. Tradition and dilettantism guide his existence with the discretion of an intelligent pen. The marvel lies in the ability to live in touch with contemporary psychology, with its drinking bars and its music halls, to keep one's mind open to new ideas, to cross the seas like a homeless vagabond.

At the lycée at Chateauroux, as in the general examinations and at the École Normale, Giraudoux was always among the first. He is well versed in both Greek and Latin. "Latin is the language to which I owe most," he declares. And his deep and wide learning does but strengthen his delicately original mind. Each of his novels is a little encyclopædia. He has lived in England, in Russia, in America, he was a professor in Germany; he has travelled all over Central Europe. The newly created map of Europe delights him. Its mixture of races, its contact of international mentalities, the foreshadowings of the future fascinate him. People call him "an aristocratic cosmopolitan" . . .

This wide knowledge, this distinction of character and intellect, go side by side with a temperament sensitive in the extreme but always held in and wearing frivolity as a mask. The entire work of Giraudoux is a school of sentiment. Affection and "*pathétisme*," memories of childhood, the witchery of spring, . . . It was thus he was led to speak to me of the heart, of friendship, of love, and no one surpasses him in the delineation of the young girls of to-day, intelligent, well-educated, and wearing their hair short. . .

Realism in his case is not divorced from poetry. Let us avoid sensuality, experience the loving camaraderie of school-days, elegant flirtations, with distinction, taste, delicacy, all the elements of a friendly gaiety. Vivacity which is now youth and sunshine, the gracious nonsense of love . . .

Sarcasm, penetrating reflection, tenderness: the kindly virtuosity of his wit, gleams always from the eyes smiling through the tortoiseshell-ringed glasses.

Dressed in a pleasant brown suit, Giraudoux is a model of simple, correct elegance. His room seeming at first so modern in tone with its varnished wood and well-chosen rugs is presently found to contain a collection of antique furniture, amaranth and mahogany tables, gilt-bound books, tenth century enamels and Florentine paintings.

A gay witticism, a quick sally after a merry tale, reveal the true character of this thinker, so French in his mind, who pretends merely to play with life because he is in search of only charming, bewitching impressions just as he collects the flowers of his herbal.

Suddenly his brow darkens. Are we going to talk politics? No. He tells me of his literary preoccupations. "To-day the writer addresses a new public which includes women, schoolteachers, many people of enquiring minds, hungry for knowledge, and also foreigners. One must therefore try to amuse while one is teaching and one must be lavish with the substance of classical tradition." And when he proceeds to regret that he writes a novel in less than four weeks, with too great facility, I remind him of his title of Prince of the School of the Quai d'Orsay . . .

On his smooth and shining writing-table I see a Chinese ruler, a mah-jong set in mother-of-pearl and other quaint objects. I note too a phonograph, while on the mantelpiece the Roman emperor, obeying a gentle pressure from my host moves his head backwards and forwards . . . The atmosphere of fun has returned. The fun of Marcel Proust, the fun we meet again in André Maurois and in Francis de Miomandre and whch leads to a joyous optimism. From this point onwards we feel ourselves in an imaginary world which is not separated from the world of reality. . . . .

63

FRANÇOIS MAURIAC

FRANÇOIS MAURIAC

Why should we trouble to unveil a figure so familiar? Why seek out in his own home this fragile, invalidish man, this "buried heart" (his own phrase) whose beatings have moved us all so much? Do we not know all about his childhood in the provinces, about the religious traditions in which he was brought up, about his college life, and about his restless youth, with its sensual romanticism and its vagabondism? The Bordeaux vineyards, one brother a priest, the other a doctor, the inexpressible poetry of the Landes pinewoods. This nature, at first passionate and violent, then crushed, languishing or starved. The Barrés-like mood of meditation, the feverishness and the despair. The obsession with flesh, so often recurrent—is it not our own? Why should we go in search of the secrets already revealed to us?

For it is François Mauriac's strength that he is able to give himself to us completely in his novels. He writes them with his own blood, with his own nerves. Our alarm in the presence of those cries, that naked pathos should not deceive us. This face, always the same. Jean-Paul or Thérèse, adorned or disguised; this unchanging temperament. "Autobiography," the reader concludes. François Mauriac denies it definitely: "I am not any one of my heroes," he has said to me. It is only when we have read all the books that we are able to disentangle what is biographical from what is romance in this blend of romance and biography.

Of a surety, a curious tendency to recoil, an anxious attitude towards life, a propensity to reveal evil, and, as a consequence, much sadness. Acuteness of impressions, flights of imagination, terrors. Exacerbated sensitiveness. Sensual excesses. These are the sources of the marvellous gifts which make him one of the most powerful writers of fiction since the War. His talent as poet, as regionalist, as an analyst of different social strata, finally, as a psycho-analyst, ceaselessly stalking the soul in order to outwit his thirst of the ideal, to satisfy his need of emotions, to penetrate as deeply as possible into the very essence, the complex essence—the passions: "Le Baiser au Lépreux," "Genitrix," "Le Fleuve de Feu," "Le Désert de l'Amour" . . . books marked of a ripe maturity and an achieved craftsmanship.

There are strange notes in his personality. The musical inflections of his voice recall the South of France. His language is marked by provincial words, words from the province to which he owes so much: "It is indispensable to have a corner of the world to which our memories are tied, in which one can immerse oneself from time to time," so he said to me, but he has cruelly gone back on this in "La Province." His delicately shaped hands are in torment, joined together as though in prayer.

"A Catholic writer of fiction? Less and less. A writer of fiction should have no restrictions upon his enquiries into knowledge of the passions. He must describe them as he sees them." There is question already of putting all the work of the author of "Destins" on the Index. He is not frightened by this threat.

It is in truth an astonishing experience to watch the evolution of a Catholic becoming a renegade The grace he entreated remains deaf to his appeals, the obsession of his passions carries him away into pursuit of the flesh. A few awkward seminarists are to be met with in his novels still. Soon religion will have no place in them at all. "Thérèse Desqueyroux" recalled the equivocal Madame Lafarge; the dubious Bob Lagave of "Destins" is a first landmark, backed up by an essay of justification, "Le Roman."

The indifference of this man, the sombre light in his eyes, the reticences of his compressed, evasive lips, conceal a bitterness which is in keeping with all his work. He takes a frigid pleasure in suppressed passions, in painful misunderstandings, in purity drowned in floods of filthy water. Mud spattered over life, over the soul. He never loses sight of this animal within us pushing us on into debauchery . . .

"The writers of my generation labour under the influence of André Gide, Freud and Proust," he once exclaimed suddenly, and it is not with voluptuousness that he speaks of the maladies of sensuality.

He suffers from desire, from the fatality of temptation, from a haunting fear of demoralization and death. From conflict with tradition, with the family, he passes on to disintegration and to pathology. In the young he finds this disorientation at its extremest. What confusion and what distress are revealed in "Jeune Homme," where one "of a horrible class of old inconsolable adolescents" attempts to discover himself again in his young flesh. This young man with his doubtful cravings, his heroisms and his basenesses, his kisses and his tears—is he not the type momentarily recalled to that stifling atmosphere in which despair pants intermittently? Chastity, before a Jansenest Christ, with arms folded. Poetry of wax candles and incense. . . .

Leaving the writer in the pleasant framework wherein he has settled down, in a home which he wishes to have tranquil and patriarchal, I touch with my finger the antinomy existing between his actual life and that depicted in his novels. The writer concentrates on his work, meeting few people, avoiding the music-hall and the cinema. A terrible sensibility, languishing, shattered, puerile, suddenly in revolt. A personality beyond question disturbing, distinctively adapted to literature. Faring in the vain pursuit of love, as do so many of our kind, hollow-cheeked, miserable ashamed . . .

ANDRÉ MAUROIS

ANDRÉ MAUROIS

Let us hie back to·civilization. Let us abandon the Freudian forest of François Mauriac for the garden walks of the author of "Ariel." English garden walks, lined with boxwood, embellished with statues, well raked, well adapted for our comfort and enjoyment. His moral attitude is happy and civilized. There is less of fantasy, less of literary embroidery in his work than in that of Jean Giraudoux. Maurois professes a mild enthusiasm of the kind appropriate to a fox-hunt or a game of bridge, a compound of serenity and wisdom. The tempests of passion do not rage round his head, his education rules out extravagance. The style which he has deliberately chosen resembles conversation of the best order. In his dexterously composed books a flavour of frivolity and elegant humour lends spice to the flow of sentiment; a trace of melancholy broods over them; the thought is clear; and a fine spirit of humanity graciously pervades them.

You should have a liking for old English prints, a relish for the romanticism of 1830, a taste for refined companionship, to appreciate Maurois. The charm of "Bernard Quesnoy" escapes those who live in clogs. Women of culture read him with delight. The windows of his ground-floor drawing-room open on a lawn surrounded by plane trees. The dining-room and library combine with this drawing-room to constitute a long stately gallery. A trifle stiff. Shining parquetted floors. Not too much furniture. Several photographs, all of the same feminine face.

To contrive to see clearly, to contrive to make intelligible what was confused—the author of "Dialogues sur le Commandement" has set himself these aims. He has sought in it also to be rational, to create himself anew, and to master the right tactics of living. He bears on his coat-of-arms those devices of the *haute bourgeoisie*, the idea of order and method, the idea of loyalty. Correctness is a possession of his family, an Alsatian family of industrialists settled at Elbeuf. His mind has been purified by the teachings of Alain, who was his professor at Rouen and under whom he attained his *licence de philosophie:* "I intended," he says, "to become a professor of philosophy." Ten years of professional and industrial work were an almost compulsory effort in the realm of action. Solitude which left him free to perfect his intellectual development, to familiarize himself with the classics, with French literature, and with the literature of England with which he had made acquaintance on a visit to Oxford. The shuttle was working out the web of his future.

The idealist who left school a Socialist found painful confirmation for his theories in a factory. The sentimentalist learnt at his own expense the value of the system of rationalism for which he had opted. Did he not encounter these same frictions and set-backs in the romantic and tender existence of Shelley? The greater part of the work of Maurois expresses a personal experience: the difficulty of applying our logic to life. "Ni Ange, ni Bete" is the transposition of the story of Shelley which he was to tell with such success in "Ariel"; and "Disraeli," a model of its kind, an admirable fragment of English political history, retracing the life of the famous statesman, is the record of the ceaseless struggle of a man of action in a hostile universe.

"The way in which a man comes into contact with the world is what interests me most. In biographies as in novels, I introduce various individuals, men of letters, politicians, women . . . and I contemplate their years of apprenticeship; that is to say, on those years in which arbitrary ideas are tried out, disintegrate, and gradually becomes transformed."

Biography for André Maurois, who has renewed the art in France by means of a system of minute documentation, is a bold research into the truth; a work of art and a means of expression: "Aspects de la Biographie" is a book which will live. . . .

His low voice, sometimes a mere whisper, is at moments metallic. . . . He does not take easily to the exceptional. "A subject like that

77

of Byron is difficult for me, because I have in me no passion, no fever." He advances his head, his features are a trifle Satanic. There is kindness in his large eyes. . . . Calculating, confident, perfect in his manners, he represents a higher class of society, that favoured few who stand for decency and decorum.

The shaven lawns of England were bound to attract him. A channel is quickly crossed. The British mentality, British reserve, British humour, British comfort, accorded entirely with his tastes. He came to know them in 1914, for he was a liaison officer and saw the War through in the company of British officers. "Les Silences du Colonel Bramble" and "Les Discours du Docteur O'Grady" embody a number of very witty stories and are the outcome of a joyous comradeship. England has supplied Maurois with themes for six of his books. The University of Edinburgh accorded him a D.LL. Trinity College, Cambridge, invited him to deliver a course of lectures. "I often spend my holidays in England," he says, "in the neighbourhood of Kipling, for whom I feel a great admiration."

A feminine grace goes with Maurois' liking for sport and music, his *honorabilité* and his *savoir-faire*. His novels are full of very polished personages and his women are their most delicate adornment. . . . The story-writer who never takes

his eyes off the fragile barque of love, who
watches the swayings of the heart, who scatters
smiles and indulgence, whether it be Francis
James or Giraudoux or Miomandre, follows
in the track of these mocking and gracious
apparitions. André Maurois makes incarnate
in them the mysterious and beneficent forces
scattered over the universe. The powerful
orchestration of "Climats," by its moderation,
its tenderness, and charm bathes the sorrows of
the heart in veneration for a woman's face.

Magic of tone and of style. His ivory hands.
His wish to please. He is civilization itself. He
wishes to be understood and is at pains to be as
limpid as crystal. . . . Death itself is softened.
He has an idea for a novel of complete love: "In
it I shall set forth my doctrine of love."

PAUL SOUDAY

PAUL SOUDAY

There is a well-accredited legend. That of a redoubtable *mousquetaire*, always ready for a fight, straddled upon a great bony old horse, cock's feathers in his felt hat, brandishing his sword, and off to a battle with the windmills: Paul Souday.

It is not without a tremor that one pulls the bell at his house in the rue Guénégaud, a few yards from the Institut. But the surprise called forth by his surroundings drives away all feeling of fear.

The ante-room is sombre, in spite of its immense mirrors, in which you see yourself reflected full-length, and its wealth of Venetian glass. It is packed full with books and curios and art treasures. A gilt statuette of the Virgin in wood stands by the door into the salon, while high up above the mirrors hang a number of portraits of distinguished personages of the *Grand Siècle*, severe-looking in their worm-eaten frames. The door opens. Behold the salon itself. A magnificent apartment. The yellow silk hangings, embroidered in gold, an imposing chandelier. Dignified, impressive furniture, consoles and tables of marble, tapestry-covered armchairs, sumptuous church candlesticks, a screen made of mirrors. And on the tables, stands and glass-cases full of all kinds of old-fashioned but charming objects: fans, snuff-boxes, porcelain flowers, ivory knick-knacks, Spanish figures of the Madonna, old-world candlesticks and snuffers, busts, old bronze lamps with pale rose-coloured shades, a bishop's mitre embroidered in gold . . . On the walls pier-glasses, any number of miniatures, engravings and candelabras. Brocades. A guitar . . A museum, in fact, wherein mingle the parade of the eighteenth century and the majesty of religious ornaments beneath the dim light which enters from the lofty windows with gilt fastenings framed by heavy red curtains.

Now the fumes of a pipe. The great critic comes in.

It is two o'clock. He has not lunched. A messenger has just been to fetch his article. His hair, becoming grey, is disordered, the collar of his shirt is open, he is barefooted in his slippers. His small white hand holds a long pipe of black clay which he puts occasionally to his lips. He takes up his position in an armchair. Now I see only a face lit up by two alert eyes above a pointed nose, a moustache, an imperial, and the amplitude of the unbuttoned jacket surrounding the big belly which is shaken every now and again by a burst of laughter. The habitué of La Régence is very debonair and very human. A quarrelsome Mousquetaire? Not a bit of it.

He is fifty-eight and he is a Norman. The sculptor Marius Cladel has recently done a bust of him. Born at Havre in 1869, he made his studies at the Lycée Henri IV in Paris, whence he went to the École Normale. But he left it to devote himself to literature and led the joyous life of a Sorbonne student. He made acquaintance with Verlaine and with Moreas, whom he calls his "*maitre et ami*"; he took a part in the Symbolist movement; then he launched out in literary journalism, made his *début* in the *Rappel*, and became a contributor to the *Temps*. He writes for it still after thirty-five years. His newspaper work brought him into touch with Renan, Zola, the Goncourts and Taine. He went in for political journalism as well. The *Gaulois*, *l'Eclair*, *l'Opinion*, *La Revue* published critical essays from his pen. Since 1912 he has been the leading literary critic on the *Temps*. He is a great worker, reading everything, interested in everything. "I love poetry and philosophy best," he declares. Among his books are "Les Livres du Temps," a collection of articles, a study of La Rochefoucauld, and one of Voltaire. Quite recently he has issued three little volumes through Kra on Proust, Gide and Valéry, and one entitled "Romantiques a l'Académie."

"Is our epoch worse than that which preceded it? No. Nor is it any better. There are at the moment a great many charming talents at work, including some of real distinction, such as Paul Valery, Henri de Regnier, Meyerson the philosopher, Gide, Claudel, Madame de Noailles, Gérard d'Houville . . . I am talking only of writers of fiction. Besides, there is no reason why any particular epoch should bring forth actual geniuses . . . In criticism? From time immemorial it has been said that there is no criticism: there have always been malcontents, namely authors. To-day we have excellent critics who have read and reflected, whereas the Boulevardiers of fifty years ago were not worth much. I shall point merely to Bidou, Chaumeix, Thibaudet, Jacques Boulanger, Pierre Brisson, Dubech, Gérard Bauer, young Leon Pierre-Quint, André Thérive, Kemp, Loweel, and Vandérem, who has the gift of working the public up into enthusiasm, but who sometimes is given to paradox. These are merely the professional critics, for Henri de Régnier and Descaves are very good critics too, although criticism for them is only a side issue. They are all benevolent towards our authors, especially towards the young. They vie with each other as to who shall discover the budding genius. Sarcey was an eminent critic, but how hard he was on the young! I read them all, these young authors, and when I receive a book the author of which is unknown I try always to find whether he has talent. And yet you know how I am deluged with books."

"But is not our criticism affected by politics?"

"So far as I can see, only *l'Action Française*. And if Maurras says that Pierre Benoit is a great writer, he says so, not because he approves of him or admires him, but because they are in the same camp. Apart from that our criticism is independent. I am accused of being a politician when I praise Claudel or Jammes or Forain or Vincent d'Indy, although they are far from sharing my ideas. As a matter of fact politics bore me. I have never really gone in for politics—only in the Dreyfus affair, when I took a strong line on the side of freedom of mind as against the principle of authority."

Paul Souday's vigour and aggressiveness are proverbial. I tried to draw him out.

"I have always fought against exaggerations," he declared, "but without anger. I took the standpoint of good sense. The cinema? A very good form of entertainment, but I have no time for it. To talk of the cinema, however, as the supreme art is folly, and the philistines who do so are not genuine in what they say. Sport? I adore sport. I used to play cricket and football, and I rode a lot. But what rubbish it is to talk about the defeat of a boxer as though it were as great a calamity as a lost battle in a war!

"So it is too with the Abbé Brémond and pure poetry. After the Abbé had delivered his address

I gave my views on it in the *Temps* in very civil language. Immediately he went for me and began to insult me. The debate became envenomed. It has ended by his admitting that pure poetry such as he talked about is a thing impossible. He admits that I was right."

But there was no real vehemence in this defence. He remained good-humoured and serene. "It is not merely in the field of modern machinery that progress is to be looked for," he went on, "but even more in the field of the mind. I am all for the intellect, for the humanities, for Greek and Latin. And I am thought to be anti-clerical! I merely stand up for freedom of thought."

At the Academy, on the day of his reception, I saw him dressed in sober black, his hair smoothed across his forehead. He was carefully got up. There he was, the "man of the world," whom we all know. He is seen out a good deal, in truth. "I am a sociable man," he admits. He loves good cheer and amusing talks. He is a ladies' man. He is a conversationalist of note and is in great request.

A protagonist of the Press, he has done battle with Thibaudet and Vandérem and Vautel. Literature is his passion. Paul Souday holds the balance—and the whip.

As he led me amiably towards the staircase, he pointed out to me the immense piles of books that are gradually squeezing him out of his study and even out of his spacious salon. They stood heaped up even on his dining-room table. His lunch was waiting for him and his plate had had to be slid into its position between two great walls of books.

II

THE UNTAMED ["*LES FAUVES*"]

JOSEPH DELTEIL

JOSEPH DETLIEL

The tones of Joseph Delteil's voice, sharp and rough and with a Southern accent, ring out clearly in the narrow dining-room which serves as his study. There are no pictures or glass cases, but pinned to the walls: drawings, photographs, postcards, maps, fantasy by Touchagues, a study by Delaunay, a wax design by Vidal-Salisch; on a blank sheet of paper the imprint of the palm and fingers of a hand, on which one may admire the line of life and the line of the heart: it is the hand of the writer, read by the clever Maryse Choisy.

In this gay and Bohemian milieu, an authoritative head, surmounting a slender body. There is a touch of gold in the chestnut-coloured hair, just as there is a gleam in the brown eyes. Through the window comes the sound of a hurdy-gurdy. There is a travelling fair encamped hard by, with its swings and merry-go-rounds . . .

Joseph Delteil was born at Pieusse, near Limoux, where he learned to become a keen angler. From time to time he deserts the Boulevard de la Chapelle, takes the train home, seizes his rod, dons his straw hat and proceeds with long strides, his countenance radiant, towards the Aude, a cool river full of fish. That homeland of his is as bleak as the Sierras of Spain. It is a region in which the heart is soon inured to the hardships of life. As a boy he lived amidst the sounds and the odours of his father's farm: it was an open-air boyhood, full of sunshine and health, of milk and apples. Neither his father nor his mother knew how to read or write; like them, he was to be a peasant of France, but the fates decided differently. The fates? No, for he does not believe in them. He believes that he holds his destiny and the control of his life in his own hands.

A man of impulse, Joseph Delteil, capable of a thousand madnesses, always independent, owing nothing to anyone. His novels are bold, joyous, full of colour; they show a generous heart, a heroic heart, and a heart that has a relish for life in all its forms however trivial. Perhaps the secret of the author of "Jeanne d'Arc" is that he is a Romanticist first, then a Rabelaisian. He exalts the riches of passion, the forces of instinct, and his pages are vibrant. But he likes to eat and drink, also, to make love and to write verses, and to fight: his lyricism has led him into every manifestation of life. Life for him connotes above all the key of the fields, sex and revolution, it comprises at once the gentlest shades of colour and and the lightest foam.

One fine day he made a new departure. He threw himself on the subject of Joan of Arc. He has sung the *poilus*. He is masculine, he has Delteilized La Fayette. Presently, no doubt, he will choose Napoleon or Adam. His boldly sketched pages have sometimes a crudity which dazzles like the sun when it is too brilliant.

Joseph Delteil explains to me that literature for him is but a momentary outlet. "Like Rimbaud I shall cease to write the day my reason dictates to me another task." If he is an individualist and an extremist. "I always ask myself the wherefore of things," he declares. "I try to understand with the best of my intelligence."

PIERRE DRIEU LA ROCHELLE

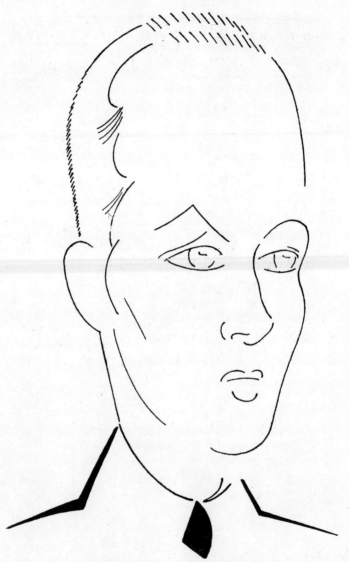

PIERRE DRIEU LA ROCHELLE

Two halters thrown down beside the sofa. An immense writing-table. Where are the punching-ball and the expander? Severity is the note of this attic without ornaments, in the verdant quarter of the Parc Monceau in which the young editor of "Derniers Jours" makes his home. He is dressed in a suit of English cloth, with mahogany-coloured shoes of thick leather. Active and supple, his athletic frame is shaped by outdoor sports, but has the slimness of young Oxford. . . "I have been a good deal in England," he says, "and have gone in for all kinds of games. I still swim a good deal."

There is something child-like in this big, blonde, blithe countenance; the head is well set on the square shoulders. An Anglo-American profile. A straight look in the very blue eyes. A delicate mouth with well-shaped teeth, a delicately shaped chin also; a high forehead; chestnut-coloured hair cut so short as to be scarcely visible. The muscles of the face are mobile. They frequently contract and relax; and suddenly the pointed ears, the arched eyebrows and the lips seem to combine in a smile in which there is something of the simplicity and of the mischievousness of a young faun. I am surprised by the suppleness of his gestures and the friendliness of his face. Have I not read of his "aggressive outbursts"? Is this not the man who wrote "*Je me livre corps et âme a l'hystérie*"?

It seems there have been three phases in his existence: the War, the post-War, and to-day.

The War tore him away from his studies and his readings and threw him into the torment; it taught him the nothingness of the universe, the suffering of the flesh, meditation, making a warrior of him. Then he aspired to be *"une homme dur,"* upstanding and strong; his imagination, his youthful need of an ideal, his thirst for heroism, found a purpose: the War brought to flower in him the strange explosive lyricism of the poems of "Interrogation" and of "Fond de Cantine."

After the chaos of the War came the post-War anarchy. It was propitious to the intellectual disorder produced by over-excited nerves. Drieu sought the fever of battles; he found it chiefly in sexual passion. He threw all his frenzy into "Etat Civil," "Plainte contre Inconnu," and "l'Homme couvert de Femmes." Impetuosity, froth of youth of a young god escaped from the Hell of the War to fall into the Hell of the senses. Disgust soon followed, then impotence. "La Suite dans les Idées" enables him to set forth his weakness: "I am not a man . . . and I have killed my appetite."

He says: "What I have written does not satisfy me. I have written books, but not yet *a* book." Recalling his political studies, he has shown what he can do as a logician and essayist: "Mesure de la

France" is an analysis of French civilization. So is "Le Jeune Européen." In *Les Derniers Jours*, his periodical, he deals with the problems of capitalism. His next book will be "Confessions d'un Français." Meanwhile he remains a writer of fiction and is working at a new novel.

"I am not at all a partisan of violence as you seem to believe," he assures me. "A writer cannot be violent; the violence of Barrès has always shocked me, that of the *surréalistes* is ridiculous; as for the energy of Montherlant, see what it has come to! I am finishing a chapter, 'Le Sang et l'Ancre,' in which I am trying to define the balance that is to be reached. But one has to guard against this bad romanticism which causes a writer to speak of nothing but himself and which makes him believe he is depicting mankind in general although he is very far from being a normal type."

This Barrèsian "moi" is precisely that which is most personal in the work of Drieu. Masculine in character, sober and frank, very attractive, for all the irregularities and the weakness of his work. In his capacity as a writer he hesitates between the novel, the Claudelian poem, and the essay, without being either a novelist, a poet or an essayist. He is not a politician, and the logician oscillates between Capitalism and Communism. All his sympathies go to the Aragons, to the Bretons . . . and he detests them. He would like to be strong and he attacks every form of weakness. But these outbursts give him an accent of persuasive force. . . invectives.

Fresh eyes, of a fresh century in which everything needs to be created anew. . . Drieu la Rochelle is one of those who rush forward towards a nascent world. He sharpens our outlook and stands at the cross-roads, a pilot to the young generations.

HENRY DE MONTHERLANT

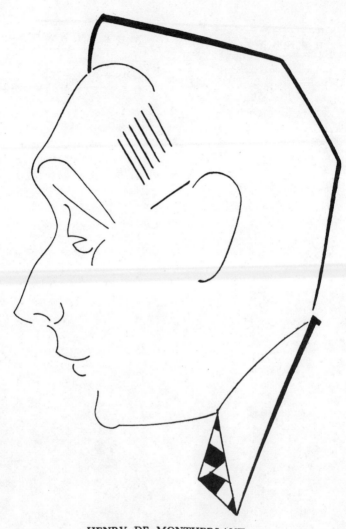

HENRY DE MONTHERLANT

Henry de Montherlant, having burnt all his most cherished possessions, has not left it open to me to so much as touch a cinder of them all. Before setting out on his latest expedition, he destroyed all his pictures and papers, smashed up his furniture, sold his books, thus cutting himself free from the moorings of the past.

On his doorstep I stood waiting to see the author of "Fontaines du Désir," the new Chateaubriand, the new Barrès, the impetuous Caesarian, child of the Sun and of Mithra, the matador overthrown but yesterday in the arena. The hangings on the wall are probably on longer emblazoned with trophies of arms like towers on a background of flashing swords. Where are the trophies of war, the running shoes, the toreador cloaks, and the portrait of Jacque-Emile Blanche, presenting the young writer so naturally against a background of Roman ensigns and eagles borrowed from the representation of Caesar's triumph at Mantegna?

I recalled the years of wealth, followed by the lean years. Years of moral force, of great effort, years of the pathetic singer of the heroic life and of the soul. Imperishable works of the morrow of the War which made Henry de Montherlant the foremost and most triumphant of the young writers of the day. Alone he professed the pursuit of all that elevates—the male virtues for the growing generation. . . Haughty, brusque, passionately inclined to grave speculations as to lyrical effusions, braced up by his nerves yet yearning for the absolute. . . .

His literary talent is exceptional; he knows how to speak to souls. His impetuosity he derives from Epictetus and Claudel. The anniversary of the day when Rome was founded saw him born under the Zodiacal sign of the Bull. An amazing youth, revealed to himself at the age of twelve by Greco-Roman antiquity. "The writers of Greece and Rome have all my life been my masters."

. . . Faure Biguet has written a perturbing little brochure, "Montherlant Homme de la Renaissance," in which he describes him slaughtering rats, half-strangling a professor, rushing into a football scrimmage impelled by brutality, slaughtering bulls voluptuously. . . Foretaste of the sadistic horrors of "Le Songe" and of "Bestiaires," and of his declarations to Frederic Lefèvre on his bestiality. "It is the repressed instincts that poison him," Faure Biguet declares; but he himself maintains in his books that "one must go to the end of oneself," that in his own case the thirst for blood and sensuality rules him and that he gives way to it without restraint.

What has not been said of Montherlant? He has been the great man of criticism, borne aloft upon a shield.

In his mystical frenzy, as in so many other of his attributes, he derives from Barrès. An ornament and glory to the religious college in "La Relève du Matin," glory of intellectuality, of courageous meditation, of pride beating dolorously against our inability to bind closer our souls. Pagan and ideologist glory of sport and of war. Glory of the stadium, triumph of the men of rude force in "Le Paradis à l'ombre des Epées" and in "Les Onze devant la Porte Dorée"; of the war, in "Le Chant Funèbre" and in "Le Songe," of the toril and blood in "Bestiaires." A strong style, in full relief; virtuosities of language, hymns, transports; odes in prose the loftiness of which very often approaches the sublime. Philosophy of unbridled individualism, insolent, borrowing its restraint from antiquity, from religion, and above all from "*la grande vie physique*."

Magnificent Catholic promise, it was said. A complex and Italian soul, it was recognized afterwards, and reservations were made. Odious aberration was the judgment after "Les Fontaines du Désir" and after a certain conversation with Lefèvre. . .

He grew tired of sport, the War was forgotten. Launching out in pursuit of pleasure, he fell into the excesses of an immeasurable egoism with which all went down. His zest for life, piqued by the needle of cynicism, intoned a chant which exalted moral depravation, the eternally romantic glittering of the senses, followed by disillusion. Spiritual bankruptcy "without remedy" . . .

October, 1928. A transformation. The flame leaps up from the ashes. A regenerative sacrifice. Like the Phoenix he is reborn, spreads his wings, and takes flight.

" 'Aux Fontaines du Désir,' six years of profound reflection, the result of which is this statement of the puerility of intellectual values: all that is not enjoyment is secondary. The title 'Sans Remède' has little appropriateness because my book is more Epicurean than desolate; it provides for possibilities: the Ecclesiast says that all is vanity, but "Hors la Joie" . . . This is the happy period that has begun for me. Of this recent experience I shall speak in my forthcoming book, 'La Petite Infante de Castille'."

Henry de Montherlant is the most charming man in the world. A certain look of rude health about his chest and neck and forehead is natural to the sportsman, the champion 100 metres' runner, the football player, and the horseman. A hatchet face, with ears which stand out from the cropped head. His body is healthy, supple, elegantly attired. The arch of his slight eyebrows, his curved nose, the lines of his mouth, all point to character and distinction. . . recalling plump cheeks, heavy eyelids. Violence slumbering beneath: *"la violence. et la sensualité sont tres importantes chez moi,"* he says. But his exterior and his method of speech have an intelligent freedom, a restrained good-sense, a *camaraderie*, which dispose of whatever conception one might have had of him as the sanguinary *vaquero* who has sucked dry the fountains of desire. No fatuity, no presumption of the boy who in short breeches and under the eye of his governess once forsook the recreations of his age in the Bois de Boulogne to compose a romance of the days of Nero : *"Pro una Terra."*

One is amazed by his vitality, his candour . . . "I sometimes receive letters from young people who ask me if they should throw up all hope and kill themselves after 'Fontaines du Désir.' I reply to them: 'You must not attach so much importance to all that!'" And under the influence of the tonic of Montherlant, who, while speaking, made me go downstairs with him, and walk along the street, and board a taxi, and enter Grasset's, still talking of this and that, I could not help putting before him the enigmas which burdened me: enigmas of the "Montherlant Case," a case at once religious and Barrèsian and moral.

"I was very religious down to 'Bestiaires'; to-day I have a keen antipathy to everything that smacks of the cassock. If I had children, I would keep them away from the priests. I deserve to be put on the Index, I see that. . . Looking backwards I blame my self for having mixed Catholicism up with sport and with the War. . . they are dissimilar notions. . ."

"Barrès?" The greatest writer assuredly of the last forty years but one who did not completely fulfil his mission as a lucid spirit. He did not tell *all* the truth, he was disloyal because he was afraid of ruining his career, afraid of contradicting himself after he had chosen his party. He was only half of himself."

"My attitude henceforth? I don't wish to adopt any other rule than that of Pleasure, Pleasure engendered by Beauty, Love and Poetry—which means a noble enough form of pleasure! . . ."

RACHILDE

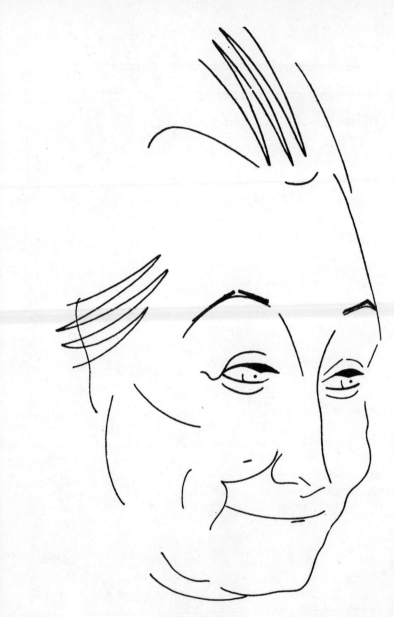

RACHILDE

An antiquated building, that of the *Mercure de France*. . . . Solemn rooms revering the patina of past centuries and where industrious silence is *de règle*. The salon of the *Mercure*, renowned for its Tuesdays, is the refuge of tranquillity and harmony in which the cult of poetry and *belles lettres* is pursued in the memory of the great who traversed it of yore and whose place is still reserved in the corner of the chimney-place. A deserted street, leading to the Odéon or to the Institute. A calm, venerable refuge.

Rachilde. "A panther that my husband is always afraid of seeing take flight!" For twenty-eight years she has not abandoned either Alfred Vallette or the *Mercure*.

"I am an old lady, I enjoy excellent health, I am always wanting to laugh. I go out tremendously, I can chatter at my ease with men, for my white hair is a super-guarantee." Rachilde laughs—nay, she roars. Her laughter bursts out like a thunderclap, roars and rumbles and reverberates. Her short, thick arms are crossed; she sits straight up, all energy and roundness and alertness, throws out a daring phrase, and laughs with all her muscular, sane face, with the white hair drawn up over it to the chignon on the top of her head in which a tortoise-shell comb is planted.

A strange, disturbing, singularly attractive face! Rachilde to-day is sixty-eight years old. She still displays all her old ardour for riding and fencing, for making mock of the law and for defending her opinions. In her villa away in the departement of Seine-et-Oise in the forest of Corbeil she heard burglars one night and she greeted them with her revolver: "I am a good shot, you know!" It is a broad face, stamped with determination, pleasantly pallid. Thick and almost black eyebrows surmount the extraordinary eyes. *Des yeux "glacés de vert, étangs mystérieux,"* Samain called them.

The descendant of a Grand Inquisitor of Spain, descended too in line direct from Brantôme, Rachilde is the daughter of an officer in the French African army. Her father shaped her character on virile lines, on his estate in severe, romantic Périgord; her mother, a silent woman, was an invalid. The house resounded with the tread of soldiers and hunters. It was thus she learnt to live, riding-whip in hand. Engaged to be married at fourteen, she tried to drown herself. She would find her way in secret to the library and try to write during the night. At fifteen she sent a short story to Victor Hugo, who replied with praise and encouragements. Soon she began to make herself known. One fine day she abandoned her family. "I left home," she says, "in the company of some Bohemians. I left comfort for years of poverty and want."

Like Mme Dieulafoy, dressed in masculine attire, she began to frequent newspaper offices and literary gatherings, had a visiting card printed, "*Rachilde, homme de lettres.*" and wrote several novels. At last, suddenly, one of them, "Monsieur Vénus," caused a scandal. Seizure of the book and the condemnation of the author to two years' imprisonment!—which, however, she did not serve. At twenty she was in receipt of compliments from Verlaine, Moréas, Barrès; Barbey d'Aurevilly remarked of her work: "Pornography, granted! But how distinguished!" Albert Samain dedicated his poems to her. Laurent Tailhade, Huysmans, Schwob, sang her praises. She married Alfred Vallette. She has written some forty novels, among them: "Nono," "La Virginité de Diana," "A mort,""La Marquise de Sade," "Les Hors Nature," "Rageac," "Le Grand Seigneur"; some plays, too, and sketches. In course of time, she opened a salon, gave receptions at the *Mercure* office (at which Carco and Dorgelès were to be met at the start of their careers) and generally played a great rôle in the world of letters.

"I am not an author for *les jeunes filles*," she declares frankly. "I am at this moment writing a book about Père Ubu, Alfred Jarry, whom I call the *sur-mâle des lettres*, and I am going to present Jarry as I saw him, an abominable creature, a thorough-going *hors-nature*, and I shall tell all I know! I am also busy on a new novel: "Refaire l'Amour," which is, admittedly, *un peu raide*, like everything I do!"

Such is this lady of letters, with her insatiable zest for the violent and the startling. . . A Romanticist by her inclination for monstrosities.

Her two hands upon her hips, she darts a wicked glance at me, then rushes off to acclaim a woman friend who has just entered the room, attired in a new Lanvin dress, opens wide her hot, misty eyes, puts out her tongue, and exclaims: "The woman of to-day is ridiculous!"

PHILIPPE SOUPAULT

PHILIPPE SOUPAULT

I met Philippe Soupault first in the labyrinth of the inner room at Kra's publishing offices. A man of the world, affable, correct. A large, long head set upon shoulders which seem hardly strong enough to bear its weight. An elongated countenance, dark, curly hair. Someone has compared his head to that of a hyena. The profile is striking, with its vanishing chin: the big front teeth give a peculiarity to his utterance which is not without charm.

I saw him again in his ground-floor flat at Auteuil, in his study, a pleasant room, full of books. Cigarette smoke, a map of the world on the wall, a piece of tapestry over the sofa. Above the mantelpiece, an old oil painting—a sailing ship out at sea. In a corner-cupboard a Crooks tube. Two water-colours by Chagall. Some photographs. A savage woman's necklace, made of shells, from Tahiti.

Soupault is seated in the centre of the room, on a stool. His expression is a blend of friendliness, irony and intellectual anxiety. There is a look of care about him, with his ascetic thinness. "We are in a state of complete, irremediable decadence," he says. "I detest our Western frame of mind—especially the French: it is that of a small clerk and bourgeois, egoistic, ignorant, maladroit in the extreme."

Even in the world of letters?

"Anatole France and Cocteau perfectly represent this spirit. The former with his writings of a Voltaire grown hollow and conventional, the latter by clownishly imitating the man of fashion, changing his style each year and claiming plaudits where he deserves to be hissed. Europe is in an intellectual mess and without realizing it is in immediate danger of being Americanized. Superficially there is a tremendous activity of the kind I have analysed in my novel "En Joue" . . . but our literature amounts to nothing.

A literary and political anarchist. He is proud of having been arrested a dozen times. He gave a thrashing to the young director of a great weekly review. He has the name of being "impossible"—a man outside the pale of Society and of the world of letters. Some people talk of him as a man of mystery, with his face in the shades. Aragon pays him a compliment: "This is the time of incomprehensible men!"

He was a normal child, born of an excellent bourgeois family, brought up in the great garden of Chaville; he was a sickly youth, as he records in "l'Histoire d'un Blanc." Education has polished him. One day everything was changed; an abyss opened on the path traced for him: a sudden discovery of freedom, pure air. Immediate rejection of the weighty bourgeois burden: "Revolt, *ma raison d'être*."

Two quite different profiles, two quite different attitudes and styles: outbursts, explosions, zigzags, and the intoxication of an epoch out of joint, whereof the cinema, the bar and the revolver are the emblems. The nervous shock of that hymn to liberty, "Le Nègre." But impotence at the same time, disgust and solitude. How sweet is the lament of "En Joue," of "Coeur d'Or" . . .

A rapid movement film, a slow movement film, in which dawns, sweet scents, memories, give forth their poetry, their sadness . . . "La Rose des Vents," with its syncopes and then, suddenly, its tenderness. Few modern writers have the sensibility, the sweetness, the endearingness of Philippe Soupault.

A dolorous sincerity; the poet's spirit takes flight upon the wings of dreams, and when an injustice or a baseness brings him back to realities he reacts in a protestation of suffering. His impetuosity sends him bounding forward like a cannon ball towards wild ventures. He is the best of friends. . .

From the moment he became a disciple of Rimbaud and Lautréamont, cast aside his weakness in a form of literature which he created, impalpable as a dream, terrifying in its plumbings of the unconscious. After the ruins of "Dada" comes the constructive work of the super-realism —that *école surréaliste* which he founded in conjunction with André Breton. The entire work of

Philippe Soupault, and in particular "Les Dernières Nuits de Paris," have this atmosphere of legend and dream.

Discovery of a supra-terrestrial poetry, negation of tradition. Intellectual fairy-lore coming to relieve the disquiet of the younger generations. Revolt against realism, scandals and extravagances of the *surréalistes*, "talking *surréalisme*," and meeting round a table, under the minute-hand of a clock, and obliged to write a page a minute, without reflection and without correction.

A strange music is to be heard in the street. Philippe Soupault rises and opens the window. A Picasso still-life: guitar and accordian . . . Two musicians enchanted our ears. He threw them two coins with a smile of thanks.

But the serenade had to cease. Life goes on. The telephone, Simon Kra, Breton. . . he was wanted. Suddenly he ran to fetch his cloak, shook my hands, jumped into a taxi . . . on his way to new destinies.

III
SENSITIVES

GÉRARD BAUËR

GÉRARD BAUÉR

I have been in Gérard Bauër's company to the sound of Jazz: it was a *soirée intime*, in the half-light of lamps and cigarette-smoke, a few of us sat in couples, silently. He himself kept moving about, dallying with the charming young ladies. His delicate fingers trifled with a cigarette. A well-cut dinner jacket, a romantic touch about his head of hair. His Italian cast of features. His indolent blue eyes, with a look in them almost scornful. His metallic voice, slow utterance, infinite gravity. An extreme distinction. The nonchalance of a poet and the frivolity of a dandy.

He is a frequenter of race-courses. He is to be seen at Auteuil, at Deauville and in Italy. I have seen him in the Hispano of one of the prettiest women in Paris. His canes, the carnation in his buttonhole, the curve of his body, have become a legend. His friendship with Paul Bourget is proverbial. He recites verses admirably. He writes proverbs, critical articles and light essays. His style is beautifully correct, academic in tone and manner. He is able to boast: "I have never asked anyone for anything." His friends are of the last century and he is only thirty-seven.

I did not get to understand him until I saw him in the atmosphere of his study, in which not a single modern book is to be found, at the top of an old building in the rue de Bourgogne. When, having donned a dressing-gown instead of his dinner jacket, he sank into the comfortable depths of a leathern armchair, he said:

"My father died when I was quite young. All he left me was twenty francs in a cup and a detestable constitution. I made my *début* as journalist on *l'Opinion*. I have known evenings when one had no dinner, only a cup of tea. By my work I have won my independence and my liberty. Having no ambition, I neglect my interests as a writer and am no social strategist. I devote myself to serious criticism; my masters are all within reach of my hand; and I earn my livelihood by walking about and keeping my eyes open in the service of letters."

A passionate devotee of literature. Gérard Bauër is a tremendous student, "having more relish for well-thought-out knowledge of the past than for ambitious creations." A disciplined spirit in spite of appearances, he is fascinated with beauty and with moral culture. If glory did not come to him sooner the reason is that, to use a phrase of Théophile Gautier's: "He loves too much that of others to think about his own."

"I am a lucid Romanticist," he said to me, as he strode up and down his vast, airy room. Art, Letters, Memories, in an immense library full of beautifully-bound books. He shows me some rare volumes, among them a Pascal, then some engravings, some framed verses by Henri Becque;

a lock of hair of the great Dumas, a sketch of
Anatole France, one of Verlaine by Cazall,
some photographs, and an affectionate letter
from Barrès, who was his great friend. . . .

Looking about me, I take in at a glance the
ensemble of books and paintings, a bit of a
frieze from the Parthenon. The furniture, the
sofa, the carpet. The big globe on his writing
table between an antique box and a collection of
paper knives. The head of a Bacchante in red clay
against the veined marble of the mantelpiece.
The small tables on which stand statuettes carved
in ivory, marble or bronze.

"There is too much specializing now and I
have not wished to confine myself to criticism. I
have sought the "*entre-deux*" of Pascal, for one
must extend the range of one's outlook. Balzac,
Stendhal, Mirabeau were so varied and yet always
the same. I write for *La Vie Parisienne;* you know
my 'Eloge du Désordre' . . ."

Badinage seems hard to reconcile with the
austere philosophic form of his weekly chronicles
in the *Echo de Paris*, wherein the moralist alter-
nates with the poet, and in which the connois-
seur of literary history and the critic, in language
fastidiously chosen, allows his thought to take
him whither it will in a form of abandonment. . .

He went on: "One must be of one's own time,
but formerly how well they knew how to suffer

for a woman!" And I understand how he regretted an epoch at which he had had only a peep—its fashions, its gallantry, its promenades in the Bois, its extravagances, its literary fervours and all its golden youth. . .

These memories came as an interruption to his vision of the post-War period, like the screen of green morocco which stood in front of the mantelpiece and attentuated the heat of a fire that was burning too fiercely. . . And the miracle lies in this: he knows how to amuse himself with the life of the day and to enjoy it rather than otherwise. . . .

PIERRE BOST

PIERRE BOST

A curious orientation characterises this young master with the Palestinian countenance, the gentle utterance and the emaciated hands.

"My biography?" Pierre Bost exclaimed to me with a smile. "I have none yet."

He was born at Lassalle in the Cevennes, of a Southern family, but was educated at Havre, and thus came to know Normandy, of which one hears so much in his books. Four years of advanced studies followed. Then a play which he had written, "L'Imbécile," was played by Copeau at the Vieux-Colombier. It was a revelation. He next tried his hand at a novel, "Homicide par Imprudence," which won him the *Prix des Amis des Lettres Françaises*. And then he devoted himself altogether to fiction, producing "Hercule et Mademoiselle," a collection of short sketches and stories; "Prétextat," a novel of Normandy life; "Voyage de l'Esclave"; "Deux Paires d'Amies"; and "Crise de Croissance," which had a huge success. In it he painted a masterly portrait of the young man of to-day.

His elocution is easy, with a certain singing tendency in it. A slight graceful figure. An oblong face, which you like to look at. Youth and animation. . .

"How can you ask me to pronounce judgment on the younger school of post-War writers?" he asked me. "Since I am one of them. . ."

"A novel," according to Pierre Bost, "should be the outcome of arduous toil." "It should be long and packed full of life, like those of Balzac. There are no such novels to-day, for our writers of fiction haven't the power."

He has expounded his own theory of literary art in the preface to "A la Porte," an early work of his, recently published. It preaches respect for rules—respect for the French language, *"un cercle ou tout le monde ne saurait être admis"*; respect for the Academy's great dictionary, that *"emouvante institution"; respect for hard work. . .*

He proceeds wisely. Intensive study has led him to recognise the eternal verities. He is not deceived: his sound judgment comes to the rescue of his sensibility. Personality with him implies talent, profound observation of actual life. He is modest in the extreme. His faculty of perception is refined by the delicacy of his constitution, and a certain pure luminosity is the result.

His work has a distinction not unlike that of Girandoux: the same unforgettable gentleness of feeling, sudden humour, lively satire. . . the work of youth on guard against "brilliance," of thought or language, against uncontrolled audacity and disorder of the senses.

His clothes are cut as implacably as those of a hero in a novel. With his natural bearing, his simplicity and cordiality, he represents refreshingly the youth of the new day.

JACQUES DE LACRETELLE

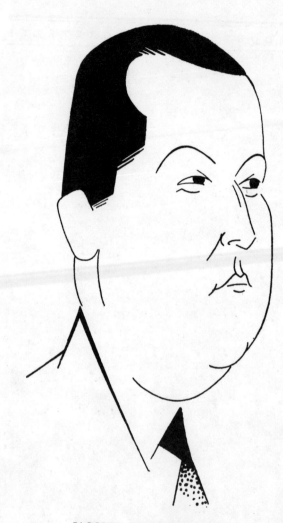

JACQUES DE LACRETELLE

Jacques de Lacretelle, who is ruled by his sense of proportion, may be defined in terms of his opposites. There are those who follow a method they believe to be personal. One will choose an extravagant formula; another, encouraging his own predilections, tortures his style and refuses to sacrifice a single idiosyncracy. With the idea of avoiding mediocrity he goes all lengths and falls into absurdity. This is a legacy of romanticism of which the super-realists are the latest heirs. It is fashionable to be odd. A saxophone in a shop window blazons forth the merit of Paul Morand's books; a skeleton on wires calls attention to those of Jean Cocteau. The writings of Jacques de Lacretelle benefit by no such propaganda. In order to consider them we must venture into an inner world. Following his own rule, the young author of "Silbermann" restrains himself, controls his instinctive reactions, and is vitalized by the self-imposed discipline. He has reached his place among the best writers of the century by dint of the exacting labour that alone can make talent effective and sustain creative power. He follows the example of the masters and approaches their level.

To point to the influence of Stendhal, Barrès or Gide is not in any way to belittle him. Every writer is another's pupil and these names do but place him. The antinomy of these three masters gives a hint of the complexity to be unravelled in a character whose personal outlines are deliberately obscured. Beneath a smooth exterior, behind luminous thoughts, we can detect half-lights, dim profundities. In his dignified first-floor on the Avenue d'Eylan, in face of his personal eloquence and cordiality, we are aware of deep-lying emotional vibrations.

Anxiety, a tendency to enthusiastic and sentimental dreaming, a superabundant impressionism seem to control his sensibility, the sensibility of "La Vie Inquiète de Jean Hermelin." An imaginative sensual warmth seems here to carry him away and is perhaps the foundation of his nature, to which he will return. After this tentative effort, a firm hand interrupts the downward flight into ardent sentimentality. His rigid ancestors, his Puritan family, his moral education and the respect he has for it, his very melancholy, all bears down upon him and develops his natural scrupulousness. These restraints incline him to the solitude he loves. He is reticent, a trifle sententious, minutely observing his own thoughts as he speaks, doubtful of himself, discreet and frank at the same time.

Thus Jacques de Lacretelle lives an in-turned life, drawn to the world only by his purpose of studying its sentiments, and passions—above all those of women. His face is superficially expressionless. A vague and sombre sadness veils the virile, almost imposing, aspect of his face and form. . . The tones of his voice are grave and metallic. And withal there is a delicate worldliness about him, a fine courtesy and distinction. . .

He is both an essayist and a writer of fiction; a lonely traveller, loving art, exile and adventure; finding pleasure in the little, unknown provincial towns to which he withdrews to work; mystical a little and inclined to the generous restrained romanticism of the XVIIIth century. His bed-book is Rousseau's Confessions. . . A tone of the moralist and the delicacy of the physician. . . "Colère" and "Le Journal de Colère" point to the man of birth, who is at once logician and of encyclopædic knowledge, with a touch about him of the misanthropist. The "Lettres Espagnoles," the "Album Napolitain," if they have a certain touch of pomp, are the breviary of the meditative tourist. The Barrèsian opposes himself to the disciple of Gide. The thinker pulls up before the spectacles which speak to the imagination, before the signs of the past, the soul of a town; he breathes in the sensations but it is not Barrès that he will ask to organise them so that he may write, like him, that "melancholy is as delightful as joy." His style is limpid. "My favourite reading is Littré."

Self-analysis, suspicion of religious origin—that of his parents—reasoned curiosity, which leads him to ferret out the furtive impulses of the soul. He knows how to lie in wait and watch. From his wanderings in Spain and in Italy he will bring back more food for thought than emotions. Nature for him is but an accessory. The Stendhalism in him predominates: "Psychology has always captivated me; even in painting I try to divine the inner meaning and the language of a portrait rather than to feel the effects of the visual impression." The author of "Bonifas," the teller of the story of "L'Ame Cachée," represses his own individuality the better to write like an historian...

His resemblance to André Gide lies partly in the Protestant orientation which they share, and in their subtle and laboured style. Adolescence interests him. The near neighbourhood of vices and virtues intrigues him, mixed up as they are in that pure and mysterious clay of which we mortals are made.

The refinement of *étude morale* and his anguished choice of subjects to which to apply it, the superiority of his talent, are the distinctive characteristics of Jacques de Lacretelle. He parcels out his days, these to life, those to work in some quiet refuge. Desires and passions surge round him. He takes flight, but returns always to his gallery of ancestors, to the engravings of all the Academicians and Lamartinians and historians and |diplomatists, whether they be benign or severe. . . .

ANDRÉ LAMANDÉ

ANDRÉ LAMANDÉ

A Gascon without cape or sword, with no accent, the stable look in whose eyes speaks of an equilibrium of body and soul. Dark eyes gazing at you through spectacles, an arched nose, delicate lips, a voice giving out harmoniously faintly malicious phrases, with just a touch of affectation. A professor of philosophy who would seem to have abandoned his philosophers for the living domain of psycho-analysis.

A Gascon proud of his Gascony, he has a relish for highly-flavoured dishes. His fingers are pointed, his finger-nails short, his supple hand is well practised with the foil . . . A vigorous man, come to full maturity. And the first grey hairs, appearing amidst the black, thick growth flowing down on one side of his forehead, enhance the authority of his mien.

On his writing-table, an untidy accumulation of papers, articles, notes, and a paste-pot dominating all. Behind him books and books and books. Assuredly he has read much and worked hard. Above his head, a bowl of dried-up mistletoe. . .

The author of "Castagnol" was born at Blaye. He has lived at Toulouzie, Payrac, Alvignac. . . He has conveyed in his work all the meridional colour of Gascony and Quercy. He did some soldiering at Bayonne, was fencing-master there. It was when he came to Paris that he wrote his verses, some of which were inserted in his book, "Sous le clair regard d'Athénée."

The War had an important influence on his development. It bathed his mind, and by its appalling blows hammered his spirit into shape. Together with the red ribbon, he has from it a moral wound which the years have not yet healed. Early in the fray, he is a contemporary of Dorgelès and Carco. . . His "Lions en Croix" is an unforgettable book. He was the first, in "Ton Pays sera le Mien," to deal with the psychological Franco-German conflict.

"I see everything against the background of the War," he said to me. In 1914 the world came to an end; in 1918 a new century began. Paul Valéry was right when he declared that the oscillation of the ship was so great that all the lamps had been turned upside down. It is for us authors to find again the lost direction and some of the eternal laws without which races and nations disappear. We must have the courage to make a choice."

André Lamandé for his part has chosen. By instinct he turns to present day subjects. . . "Lions en Croix" is the first panel of a triptych, followed by "Le Roman de l'Après-Guerre," and completed by "Ton Pays sera le Mien" and "En fants du Siècle" what discussions these books called forth amongst the critics and amongst the young!

The young! André Lamandé is drawn towards them: "They are of their time," he says, "sensitive, lucid, with a cynicism which is often but a form of *pudeur*, and a Gide-like sincerity—a sign of moral decomposition and perhaps a source of disenchantment. Good? Evil? Sin? The distinction between these things is impossible for them. They welcome all ideas and retain those especially which seem to them exceptional or abnormal. For them the only sin is in submitting to established rules. Hence their overmastering craving to destroy, no less than their constant desire to edify."

"What a theme for a novel! " I said.

"Precisely; I have just finished writing it. I call it 'Leviers de Commande'."

He smiled guilefully. A new departure for the writer who never forgets his somewhat lazy and sceptical Gascony—with its wit. To distract himself he has made a selection of "Les Plus Belles Lettres d'Amour et de Guerre du Roi Henri IV," to follow his "Vie gaillarde et sage de Montaigne," that erudite volume, so joyous that the ignorant think it all a fantasy.

Integrity. The power of a gallant man. André Lamandé seeks to move, to convince, to place the reader in a better state of mind. Is not this what La Bruyère meant by work "made by the hand of the workers"?

FRANCIS DE MIOMANDRE

FRANCIS DE MIOMANDRE

"How can one despair of a time when Jazz is dominant?" Francis de Miomandre lifts his hands to Heaven ecstatically, throwing back his head, his countenance exalted and transfigured. His eyes are raised to the ceiling. Then his voice attains unimagined altitudes as he gives forth the words accompanying the theme immortalized by Paul Valéry—"*Ah! la danse, la danse! . . . qu'importe la vie, puisqu'elle nous apporte la danse!*"

A modern Boulevardier, his trousers are the widest in all Paris—was he not the founder of the "Club des 27"? . . . He has his home, a curious home, at Auteuil. There he has written more than twenty novels, which have won him the limelight of the Prix Goncourt; there he dwells among innumerable *bibelots*. "The writings disappear, the *bibelots* remain." There he muses in the company of his chameleon, perched on a branch of a plum-tree: a creature of the moon, fragile and majestic, whom he adores; and whose greyish-green turns in the sun to white. Tomfoolery is an expression of life—life is so full of queerness: "There is nothing banal except the conventional."

In a form of frivolity all his own, he seems to have realized the "Intoxicate yourselves" of Baudelaire. Philosophy, psychological studies, subtle essays, alternating with a humour which calls forth every kind of laughter.

Pleasing predilections for all that is weak and

agreeable and mischievous: animals, dolls, dandy-ism. Unceasing renovation. Adaptation and enthusiasm, the food of youth. The times carry us along but what course is so swift as that of the author of "Ecrit sur de l'Eau," of "L'Aventure de Thérèse Beauchamps," "Le Voyage d'un Sedentaire," "La Mode," or "Les Baladins d'Amour"?

His hand is soft, his features are delicate, his eye is alert. He places all his delicate wit and all his powers of invention at the service of these expressive puppets. "Innocent pleasures," he claims, "and more philosophical after all than many others: by means of them one flies, one escapes." And the disenchantment, the resigned melancholy which you note in him tell the price of his devotion to these puppets and fetiches of every description which fill his rooms.

He once kept a vulture in his kitchen, some green frogs, some waltzing mice from Siam, a paralytic cat and two Grand Dukes. His friend, André Gide, was tenderly attached to his Dindiki. Francis de Miomandre cherished for years a little monkey from Japan, Sada, whose mutinous head would nestle in his jacket while he worked.

Does he not seem like a little seigneur of the XXth century, this elegant libertine who rhymes so cleverly, who amuses himself composing dissertations on the delights of gluttony and on the inconstancy and lovable perversity of women, who is moved and touched by the strains of the Jazz band of the "Boeuf sur le Toit," who dresses in clothes of raspberry colour, whose gallantries and affections are so delectable, the author of "Passy-Auteuil ou le vieux Monsieur du Square," that witty pastel so full of profound psychology and indulgence, and whose plays are acted at an American college for young girls? . . .

JEAN-LOUIS VAUDOYER

JEAN-LOUIS VAUDOYER

Fourth floor of an old building in the corner of the Palais Royal . . . A narrower staircase leads me up to the roof. Two low doors. Then a third which opens with difficulty. I enter a down-at-heel attic, crammed with pictures and books, lit only by a single dormer window. As I advance, a hand stretches swiftly out from behind the door to warn me of a hidden step, whilst a virile voice exclaims: "Be careful not to knock your head." I bend down just in time and make my way into the little room. I have come to pay a visit to a real-life M. Bergeret, to M. Jean-Louis Vaudoyer, artist, belated dreamer, a melancholy lover of the past. . .

A poet of wisdom and balance, a man of magnificent stature and impressive countenance. The high forehead, the bold eyebrows protect eyes that have a somewhat timid look in them. He carries his head of brown hair proudly. A fine profile for a medallion. His manners are those of a patrician. With the same scrupulous particularity he will show you a picture, buy himself a broad-brimmed hat or chisel a couplet. He talks to me agreeably about a woman and sips a *rhum martinique*, of which he cherishes the recipe He frequents cafés and enjoys a music-hall.

A man of the world, belonging to a time when elegance and wit were the rule in Paris salons. He has contrived to retain the tone of yesterday.

It was through no mere chance that he contracted friendship with Marcel Proust.

"I detest Paris more and more," he declares. "I would like to settle down permanently in Provence and only return here now and again, like the peasants who go to town only to take their poultry or their eggs to market... My house is awaiting me at Aix-en-Provence, that charming and beautiful town impregnated with the poetry of passion."

This "sedentary traveller" who used to compose while sitting outside the cafés, this last survival of the sentimental *flâneur*, wanders over the entire field of letters. He has written many novels. His verses have a delicate inspiration—

"Mes thèmes sont le ciel, l'espace et la lumière
Les fleurs que le soleil jette sur la rivière
Et sous ces fleurs de feu, les mouvements de l'eau..."

The Academy in honouring him has remained faithful to its mission...

He has exercised his artistic and literary curiosity, his delicate sensuousness in "Beautés de Provence," in "Nouvelles Beautés" and in "Saintes-Maries-de-la-Mer."

The author of "Propos et Promenades" lit a match to show me a centauress by Fromentin, then a portrait by Ricard, some souvenirs, a glass paper-weight containing multi-coloured flowers. He took down a Florentine statuette in bronze from the mantelpiece; then showed me paintings and sketches by Ingres and Jillot (who was Watteau's master); a drawing of Malibran by Delacroix; a Forain. . . mirrors, cretonnes, tapestries.

I admired above all the fire in his eyes when he described Provence and his haunts of other days, his emotion when speaking of the great masters of last century.

He passes, without specializing, from reality to poetical dreams. He is spiritually a godson of Barrès and Henri de Régnier, and he is the friend of Jean Giraudoux and of de Lacretelle.

At a curio shop he will sometimes buy, instead of a knick-knack or an old engraving, a few yards of some old stuff out of which his astonished *chemisier* will have presently to cut him a shirt. . .

IV
POETS

JEAN COCTEAU

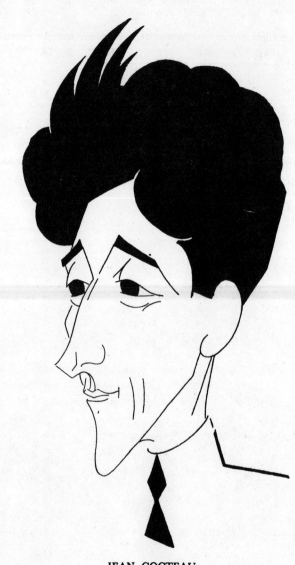

JEAN COCTEAU

Upon the screen of thought where each word evokes an image and our dreams and ideas cinematographically unroll themselves, 'J'ean Cocteau" produces a fantastic medley of impressions. Even his name suggests an extravagant design: evasive lines, light with a new grace, stark and clear, yet shocking to our good sense and missing deliberate trickery only by a hairsbreadth. He is a literary prestidigitateur, darting hither and thither, easy, airy, mysterious, flying off the moment one approaches him, along with his phantasmagoria.

His salutation, we have often seen it, is an exaggerated swift salaam, the counterpart of his nervously stiff, upright bearing. Actor and author: his face sharp and piercing, with sadly lifted eyebrows, and pallid perhaps beneath his make-up, is surrounded by a clown's crest of hair. His sleeves are always turned back as if in readiness for a conjuring trick. He never smiles. He salaams once more, with hand feverishly clasped: applause, shouts, cat-calls.

Such is the young producer of literary tempests, the *chic*, the leader of his generation's vanguard. "I do not like scandal," he declares, "but it is necessary to shake up the mutts." Dynamiting the corrupt art and the decaying literature of our period, he assails our ears with new sounds. Dishevelled poems, incredible spectacles, grotesque drawings: prodigious qualities as novelist, dramatist, poet and árt-critic, jazz-drummer, designer, comedian. He dazzles us with his glitter and it is easier to survey his mind than to enter it. His studio, full of bric-a-brac, cartoons, plasters, figurines in straw or wire, devinettes (alas, no dictionary) and paper cocottes, Greek heads, locks of hair, ships, a crucifix, reveals a man always on the look-out for the fantastic.

Jean Cocteau is like his handwriting, rapid, feverish. He cannot keep still, he shuts a window, opens a door, pulls forward a table, keeps continually on the move, pouring out talk, his countenance impassive and his mind far away. The slightness of his supple, nervous body. . . He tells me he is ill.

An astonishing talker, passing unpremeditatedly from subject to subject, but in a voice that tells of suffering, in a monotone that is never gay. . . The telephone bell rings. What a weariness . . . He goes out worried but alert. I notice a silhouette which he has done of Barbette raising a leg to heaven, and a large oil painting by him of Jean Desbordes in sailor's garb. He returns surreptitiously and, moistening a finger, he refreshes the temples of the portrait. The author of "Thomas l'Imposteur" and of "Antigone" has no apparent sensitiveness, his eyes are dark, no lips, pointed teeth. He turns this way and that, bends his knees, stretches out his hands, plays with his handkerchief and, to emphasize a phrase, touches me. .

"My very spinal marrow is in my work, and making poetry has ravaged me, robbing me an eye or a hand like the X-Rays. There are those who live by their art, who withhold themselves, compel the admiration of the public and turn their talent into money—these are the people who are believed in. The others die, give themselves entirely, and are thought ridiculous and treated like acrobats. . . These, like me, are on their way to suicide. . . Don't you find this year of 1928 a formidable year, full of mysterious happenings? . . . To-day the dreadful malaise is reaching a head, everything is becoming as solid as a knot, and a boy like Jean Desbordes astounds me. . . (so does anyone). So do Picasso or Stravinsky. . ." And he launches out with the latest film, the latest book, the latest creation of Serge Diaghilew in the Russian Ballet. . . His interest is incessantly in movement along the edge of intellectual progress. "I am not a writer," he says, "all my work has been done as an amateur."

This swift, agile, brilliant intelligence, both critical and creative, passionately absorbed in the arts, at home with them all, yesterday gave us its measure in "Le Rappel a l'ordre," and the remarkable essay on Picasso; to-day, in a study of

Chirico, Cocteau is the leading spirit of the new Bohemians amongst whom are to be found Max Jacob, André Salmon, Picasso, Stravinsky, Georges Auric, Francis Poulenc—yesterday Guillaume, Apollinaire and Erik Satie.

He disconcerts his critics, fills the young with enthusiasm and provides fresh pastures for the snobs. He is an arc lamp perpetually alight for the benefit of smart people. But he is burning himself out. One could wish him a hundred leagues away from his slavery but what would he be without it? "I never go out," he declares, "I see no one, I hate social life." Alas! One needs only to know his surroundings, to see his outfit of cosmetics and his quaint garments and attitudinizings, to hear his vocabulary and follow his thoughts, to know that he is perpetually on parade. His very life is dramatic. His exceptional qualities, the depth of his perceptions, the excitement of his many preoccupations explain this. "If I think," he confesses, "I am lost."

FERNAND DIVOIRE

FERNAND DIVOIRE

A woman of great beauty having sworn that I would see the Devil, I went hot-foot to Fernand Divoire's, eager for the experience. The door was open, a number of persons—were they demons?—were making their way in, procession-wise. I followed.

The Satanic cavern was a strange place, a long narrow passage-like room. The walls were plastered with queer paintings and inscriptions. I saw a proclamation about fishing and a prayer: "From hideousness and heaviness, good Saint Louis, deliver us!" And while I was beginning a question to the affable host these words stared at me from the wall: "*Les biophages sont des gens qui viennent inutilement manger la vie des autres.*"

A sarcastic smile had been my welcome. A keen face, pointed nose, a mordant lip; the eyes, of a very dark green and agreeably shaped, become suddenly large at moments of mystical excitement and gaze at you with a gentle tenacity, beneath the long rampart of knitted eyebrows. Complexion white and clear, projecting forehead, bald. The face runs down to a sharp point like Ronsard's, and has the anxious expression of Ignatius Loyola, clearly chiselled as though in stone, ending in a trim blond beard.

I watched him closely. Singular subtlety, poetic sensibility, masked by dominating will, are the outward characteristics of a mind turned towards spiritualist problems, a mind amusing itself in being caustic, in exploiting the allurements of its own gentleness and ferocity.

Soon I felt the charm of the fundamental simplicity, the scrupulousness of this writer who is called at once "the Christian Poet" and "Machiavelli."

Such was my original impression of Fernand Divoire, whose hands, while we talked, twisted a piece of paper nervously, and who laughed diabolically. A writer of strange verses, a practiser of occult sciences, given to humorous comments, crushing in their bitterness. But *finesse* and certainly indulgence are the real matter of the man. And if we peer into his mind, and follow his thought on its chosen levels, we shall see that his intellectual probity is equalled only by his modesty.

A great journalist and philosopher, chief editor of our foremost evening paper, continually interrupted, keeping his eye on the movements of even the least important organs of a ponderous administration, he has achieved the miracle of remaining a poet and an aesthete. But must we not reproach him for not having put into practice his valuable teaching on the subject of *la stratégie littéraire!* . . .

A Belgian, naturalized a Frenchman, he made his studies in Paris, inscribed his name at the

Faculty of Medicine, but frequented the company of poets more than that of professors. In the Quartier Latin he was often to be seen among the young and clamorous writers, heirs of the Symbolists and the Parnassians. He made a reality of the *simultanéisme* of Barzun, championed symphonic poetry and won distinction as a poet himself. "Flandres," "Poètes," "L'Amoureux," "Naissance du Poème," "Ames," "Orphée," the "Discours des Enfants," and recently "L'Homme du Monde," attest his fidelity to poetry, a poetry of his own of strange architecture, sometimes learnt from such masters as Hermesianax, Alexander of Etolia, Lycophron and, above all, Simmias of Rhodes. Poems touched with idealism, now hard and Nordic, now brilliant with diffused light. "Itinéraire,"—*poèmes "avec parenthèse"*—musical and sober, and warm, pure, like the classical chorus, graven as though in marble.

The loftiness of his inspiration shows him tormented by the eternal infinities the silence of which so troubled Pascal. And his metaphysical poetry finds its complement in the study of the soul. "Cérébraux" appeared in 1906 at the same time as his earliest verses, followed by "Faut-il devenir Mage?" and "Metchnikoff Philosophe," philosophical essays and commentaries (showing the influence of Péladan,

Eliphas Lévi or Nietzsche?). . . He defended the
immortality of the soul and dealt with the themes
of Good and Evil, and with occultism and magic.
"Pourquoi je crois a l'Occultisme" gives his reasons
for his absorption in these things.

Thus he came to the subject of the Dance and
to the writing of "La Danseuse de Diane,"
"Isadora Duncan fill de Prométhée," "Décou-
vertes sur la Danse". . . From the Dance to the
Hymn there was but a step, and this he took with
"L'Exhortation à la Victoire," the tragic chorus
performed on the Champs-Elysées in 1917,
"Ivoire au Soleil," and "Marathon," a tragic
episode.

His mode of utterance, unhurried, aims at
rendering his thought, hesitates, corrects one
word by another. Sometimes a reflection,
smiling but bitter, a pitiless piece of raillery,
recall his absolute independence and his nerves,
so near the surface and so difficult to control.
But a concentrated energy may be read in his
face and an iron will, the gift of his Flemish origin.

It is to this will that he owes his intellectual
studies and his brilliant journalistic career.
President of the *Association des Courrieristes
litteraires*, he was the first to found, in 1909, a
literary *courrier* in *l'Intransigeant*, which he has not
abandoned: a journal of capital importance
which reflects the life of the world of letters and

follows actuality in the most important of its activities, that of the intellectuals, who in all civilizations occupy the front rank. The merit of Fernand Divoire is great. Long years of perseverance were necessary before he achieved success. To-day everyone has imitated him, profiting by his initiative. During the War he founded and edited the *Bulletin des Ecrivains:* this organ was the first principle of the *Associations des Ecrivains combattants.* He organized *Art et Liberté* and *Art et Action* himself. A very finished lecturer, a critic contributing to numerous periodicals. . .

"I am finishing a novel," he tells me. His fingers travel over his brow and closing his eyes for a moment he seems to be following out a dream. But he must listen at the same time, benevolently, to his secretary, to the compositors, to the assistant editors. . . They all have to consult him unceasingly, a thousand things need his attention and his signature. . .

MAX JACOB

MAX JACOB

Francis Jammes, Max Jacob, the two poles of
Poetry; their meridian, the Catholic religion.
Their sense of uneasiness is the same, their need
of the absolute, of profundity and of purity,
their fantastic symbols; naïveté, sincerity, their
meditations; their flight from the world—the one
to Hasparren, the other to Saint-Benoît-sur-Loire,
each beneath the shadow of a church tower. But
if the former adds his name to those of Claudel
and of Henri de Régnier, in a symbolism slightly
toned down, regardful of the metres of a perfectly
formalised poetic art, the other, the disciple of
Rimbaud, of Aloysius Bertrand and of Lautréamont, affiliates himself to Cendrars and to
Reverdy. Apostle of cubism, father of *surréalisme*
and denied as such by the *surréalistes*, humorist
and satirist, creator finally of numerous new forms.
His influence will have been considerable. But
in opposition to the influence of Francis Jammes.
And nevertheless both could subscribe to this
saying from "L'Art Poétique"—"*On ne donne la
vie que par l'émotion.*"

At the end of a long gallery in which somewhat
daring pictures were drying, Max Jacob was to
be seen in the attitude of a lecturer above attentive
heads. His address was on the hidden meaning
of the anatomy of Christ. The words flowed
from his lips, slowly but easily, persuasive, in the
tone of a very accommodating professor who

speaks for those who will take the trouble to
understand. He taught the strange symbol of the
Way of the Cross and its accord with occult
sciences, the signs of Christ and those of Buddha,
the emblems of the intelligence and how theology
explains itself by magic.

Short, strong-backed, his forehead bare, his
head crowned with white locks; a full, tanned
rich countenance. Vigorous features: "I was born
at Quimper, of a Jewish family, and atheistical."
Eyes a bright grey, thoughtful, with a slight defect
in them. A monocle and a tie with wide blue
stripes, loosely knotted. A little emphasis,
infinite amiability, compunction; a "bénisseur" he
has been called. A comedian of the beau monde.
Picasso depicts him in the garb of a Roman
Emperor, crowned with laurels.

I have observed him also looking at a collection
of models of ships at the house of a friend who
received him just before his train left for Orleans,
to take him home to the cell of Saint-Benoît
where he writes his poems, his mystical verses,
where he does his pen drawings and astonishing
water-colours. A monastic life, intensely religious
and rural. "Finis, the disorder of yesterday, its
turmoil and noise, its excess of frivolity. To-day
I work in seriousness, in the very depths of
myself; I would fain do my work over again in a
lower tone—perhaps it is age that desires. . .

I have come here to work upon three operettas which I have written: their music is by Sauguet, Cliquet-Pleyel, and Roger Désormières. There I give rein to my fancies in a satire of manners. . . just as in the 'Cornet à Dés' I have depicted the *loufoquerie* of people!"

Gravity, extravagance. Between these two lies the meeting-place of the manifold aspects of his character, the place where one would like to distinguish the humorist from the psychologist, the artist, the poet, the mystic, and the "man of quality"—as Andre Salmon expressed it. A thing difficult to do sometimes, for tomfoolery and audacity have an equal part in Max Jacob— they are essential elements of his art. A dangerous, disconcerting game, whose supreme exponent is Jean Cocteau. Pretended incoherences, hetero- clite elements, puns, sometimes dishevelled cap- rices. . . The story of Max Jacob's life gives us some clue to this strange and otherwise incompre- hensible mixture. . .

After going from the lycée at Quimper to the École Coloniale, he discovered his vocation for painting and made for Paris "without baggage, without money, without even an overcoat." He earned his living at first by giving piano lessons— his first efforts at painting would not sell. Presently he met Picasso who remained his friend for thirty years. Unable to keep going in Paris he returned to Quimper where he worked first as a carpenter, then as a solicitor's clerk. Back to Paris as secretary to a barrister, he soon changed his occupation again, becoming in turn a tutor, a shop attendant, and a poet. A penniless poet at first, but success came and turned the Bohemian into a dandy. Meanwhile he comes twice to the front in 1909 and 1914. One fine day after countless vicissitudes he became a convert to Catholicism. He would not flee from the world. "Saint Matorel," "La Défense de Tartuffe" . . . He was a Christian mystic.

Incredible adventures followed. Poverty, suffering, struggle: no home, no belongings, nowhere to take root. . . Revolt, intellectual, literary and artistic, nursed in the Rue Ravignan, in conjunction with Picasso, Appolinaire and André Salmon; then the disturbance brought about by the War; new schools demanding a revaluation of values; tortured, exalted poetry, the quest of idealism.

A dual outlook now: satirical observation, resulting in such books as "Filibuth," "Le Roi de Béotie," "Le Cabinet Noir," "Cinématoma," "Le Phanérogame". . . wherein, in the light of fancy and interminable sophistries, he institutes a remarkable psychological study of the thousand and one complexities of the bourgeois mind. And violent poetry, many-hued—"Le Laboratoire Central," "Pénitents en Maillots Roses"—in which the most curious gifts are lavishly exhibited.

In "Le Cornet à Dés" and "Visions Infernales" he made prose poems in which the union of words and images, their mutual appeal and uniformity of tone are to be observed, with no regard whatever to the subject or to the picturesque, as he explains in "L'Art Poétique." In this form of prose poem Max Jacob has suppressed the intermediaries between the reality and the reverie, by introducing this latter into literature. "A re-creation of the life of the earth in the atmosphere of Heaven" he calls it. . . Dreams, meditations, the Beyond, all found their place. An event of the greatest importance, the appearance of "Le Cornet à Dés" in 1917.

The idea of the Beyond is an essential part of him. He has studied occultism and magic with passion. . . He is said to have predicted the War. It was his pursuit of mystery that led him to the Catholic religion. And after proclaiming his conversion, he wrote mystical poems where angels hovered in prayer to the Virgin. Everyone has been imitating him since. The conversions are still going on.

But to-day, wearying a little of his tragic irony, he has resumed his pencil and is busy sketching. He has exhibited at *Fermé la Nuit* evangelical visions of an ardently mystical type, water-colours which fetch high prices.

The New Testament, solar myths, the Church, illumine his speech. He knows the laws of the stars and the seasons. Everywhere almost he sees mischievous spirits about.

In his village he is called a sorcerer.

FRANCIS JAMMES

FRANCIS JAMMES

A pilgrimage of the heart. Few visits have left me such a memory as my journey to Hasparren, to see Francis Jammes. Vallon, smiling and verdant, where the rivers run, hills heralding the Pyrenees, the entire Basque countryside claims you the moment you leave the train.

The bells of the cumbrous wagons, the accents of the boys in berets, the dark eyes; the far horizon of snow-clad peaks, the simplicity of this region of France. Lourdes and Biarritz interwoven. Then the charm of the rich plain, of the pebbles borne down by the torrent, the bridge of Orthez, the ridge of Cambo, the ornamentation of a sumptuous villa in which Rostand died, the spire of the church of Hasparren—not one of the old churches of the country, so touching in their mass, and curious with their gallery reserved for men, but a new church, a church of this century, very naïve, like a statue of stucco—the maize, from which a quail rises, the hare scampering away into the distance—impressions wherein palpitate the freshness of emotion of the poet of the "Géorgiques Chrétiennes," the teller of the story of Clara d'Ellébeuse.

The consoling horizon of "*toute une France poétique*" suitable for a spoilt child like Paul Morand who, tired of rushing to the other end of the world, exclaims, disappointed: "Nothing but the land!" And a face that dominates our century, with keen eyes behind pince-nez, a square head covered with the Basque beret, a patriarchal beard, bushy and spreading, of the friend of nature, of the friend of animals, of the poet of young girlhood. Ah! the witty old fellow, the Virgilian giant, shaking under the attack of his seven children escalading him. What a restful "desert," this hermitage wherein blossoms the dream of a seeker of wild solitude!

There was a sudden sound as of something cracking on the top of a cabinet or stand—I looked about but could see nothing. It happened again, a slight, sharp sound, as of some insect at work; I went in search of it; on a desk several little cages stood in a row, fragile, Lilliputian prisons, each with a lettuce leaf, a pile of nuts and some moss, inhabited by a menagerie of crickets. Fragile little crickets with their filmy antennæ, their delicate, bent legs, ebony-black little crickets: "They know me. I have brought them up with much devotion. Natural history and botany, poetry and theology divide my life."

Poetry, inexhaustible source, the symbolism of the rustic poet, a lyric raising the soul aloft. "Mysterious virtue, which for so many centuries has surprised, astounded, disconcerted, irritated all the vulgar of the world, but which on the other hand charms, consoles, enchants, draws tears of hope and joy from all those who have a

human heart of flesh. . ." words of "Janot-Poète,"
whose sentiment has the sweetness of balm. . .

And it is by his confident heart that his whole
life is explained.

Surrender to the emotional appeal of the
beauties of nature which magnifies creation,
bestowing its bounty upon children, upon the
humble, upon the delicate souls of the young
girls whose purity caresses like that of the flowers.
Beneficence in his work and in his life, appease-
ment which gives to him the idea of a good God,
very indulgent and no doubt bearded like himself.
Thence, his seeking of souls as simple as nature,
of sweet naturalness and naïveté. A new Bernardin
de Saint-Pierre, a new Jean-Jacques, he has re-
juvenated our literature. The animals talk,
things can think—or are symbols. The "Roman
du Lièvre," the "Portraits de Femmes" . . .
supreme revel of candour, gentleness and gracious
subtlety. "La Brebis Égarée," not understood by
the mass ended by being hissed at the Opéra
Comique!

"We must rid ourselves of everything, always
rid ourselves of everything, like the saints. Man
is horribly complicated, he should be at pains to
break away, to simplify himself, until he comes
to the slender tapering line like the crest of the
mountain as seen in the evening."

And he added: "To-day I grow old but I am

nearing that crest and I see more and more clearly." Emotion marked these words, I saw his books of meditation, and the "Lavigerie" recently published. . . .

Walks in the country, the poet goes botanizing or rhyming, dreaming, hunting with the young folk of the village beyond the mountains. In his study in which a log of wood is blazing, I see his gun and game-bag. I note also an old pig-skin trunk, a guitar hanging on the wall, alongside a Torricelli barometer. Over a *prieu-Dieu* is spread an old Indian shawl, red and gold, books are piled up everywhere, a portrait of a priest. . . emblems of conversion.

Bernardin de Saint-Pierre and Chateaubriand dreamt of islands. And it is the same kind of exotic inventions, travel-tales of uncles returned from the Americas, that delight us in the books of Francis Jammes. For in the Basque country are many who expatriate themselves and who come back with gold and memories of adventure. . . . Joyous feelings, a trifle antiquated, intimate, romanesque, with the grace of Almaide d'Etremont, the tenderness in the eyes of Pomme d'Anis, and the mind ever turned towards what is good. A bucolic lyre, happily tuned to mythology. "Diane," a comedy in three acts, in the taste of the ancient Greeks, and in the highest tradition, celebrates in its verses, perfectly chiselled, Diana and Love, the Shepherds, the Gods and Beauty.

"What strength there is in verses when feeling is put into them! Poetry ought not to be formal. As to those moderns who introduce cubism into poetry, it is the negation of all, the desolation of desolations!" A bird flew past us with a cry. The Master brightened up and talked to me of his youth, of the books he is now writing, of his country avocations. . .

We rose from our seats and he whistled for one of his dogs. The garden stretched out all round the house in the shade of a grove of trees of diverse kinds. Many flowers lent brightness to the scene. With a pleasant phrase he gave us an armful of them. Alas! we had to leave him, his beard blown about by the wind while he played with his dog. And lively barks followed us as we made our way down the village road, seeming to testify that neither the poet's heart nor his jovial health were losing their young verdure; it was a hymn of gaiety, a brave greeting to the animals of the plain then sinking to sleep in the sunlight and smiling, perhaps, at the thought of the Salesian philosopher.

MAURICE ROSTAND

MAURICE ROSTAND

Verses upon verses. . . falling leaves, Alexandrines in flight. Maurice Rostand has taken poetry into the Music Hall. Between two "turns," between two spasms of Jazz, he launches upon an astonished public a seething torrent from that lyrical heart of his.

At a period when poetry looks exhausted and when poets discredited, Maurice Rostand raises his intrepid head, fronts the masses, and bestows on them the balm of his songs. This boldness, this *panache*, this dramatic attitude, and the tones of his voice, are the last stand of an illustrious art, last memory of the Masters of yester year, ultimate echo of the disciplined Muses.

A glorious name and venturesome youth were needed to enable Maurice Rostand thus to stand alone in the majesty of sublime flights and tragic miseries. He goes about enveloped in a golden legend. He gives resounding blows, passes from the theatre to the novel, creates a scandal, is challenged to fight. . . .

A fantastic figure. A strong, cheerful countenance, aquiline nose, a wild mane of tousled hair. Eyes dark brown, sombre, gentle, affectionate. Thin lips, well-shaped ears, head thrown back. The vast salon, so near the Arc de Triomphe, is still redolent of the fame of the author of "Cyrano de Bergerac" and of "Chantecler." I almost felt myself in his presence—his portraits are there side by side with those of Rosemonde Gérard and Sara Bernhardt. . . But the room is different. Less furniture in it now, fewer things on the tables, walls almost bare.

Maurice Rostand reclines in a stately Louis XIV armchair, legs crossed, displaying the strength of his body and the delicacy of his feet. He smiles. Grey suit, blue shirt. An air of well-being and ardour. Gaiety, vivacity mark his speech. Something almost childlike in his youthful charm.

He made his *debut* very young, in poetry. At eleven he won a prize in the *Annales* with a little poem: "Vacances." His first volume of verse appeared in 1908, then "Le Page de la Vie," a fairy comedy; next "Un Bon Petit Diable," and a lyrical *conte*, "La Marchanda d'Alumettes," in collaboration with Mme Rostand, his mother. In 1919, a piece in verse, "Casanova," was given at the Bouffes-Parisiens; then came his novels, "Le Cercueil de Cristal," "Le Pilori," and "L'Homme que j'ai tué."

In 1921, Sarah Bernhardt appeared in "La Gloire." "L'Ange du Suicide" and "Le Second Werther" followed; and "La Déserteuse" and "Le Trouble"; his last play, "Napoléon IV," is certainly his strongest. Its sustained action, its wealth of incidents, its national theme, all help to make it a powerful drama.

"I have just finished a novel, 'Le Vice du Siècle,' a study of the malaise of our time which is due to the lack of faith." . . .

He produced a volume of poems, "Morbidezza," prefaced by these words of Luther:

"When grain is there, I grind the grain;
When none remains, I grind myself."

"My masters? Not specially the Romantics, but Stendhal, Racine, whom I love much, the English writers and yes, above all, Musset."

An active, sociable, independent existence; the mane of a warrior. He has no fear of scandals and he speaks out. But in the face of his rich humour, his wholesome aspect, his active and brave bearing, one cannot but be astonished by his literary work with its tone of utter despair, as of a wounded heart unable to accept the world as it is and moaning over its depths of woe. Every one of his novels is the story of a suicide or of a soul in misery. Sobs, paroxysms and "*cher passé que j'aime*" of "Morbidezza." How reconcile an indomitable nature, vivid, mordant, with these imaginings?

"The sorrow of a mind which reflects. Did Musset show his sadness? And Schopenhauer, in ordinary life all fun and gaiety? . . . No, I am not an apologist for suicide and I am not responsible for the deaths which have followed 'Le Second

197

Werther.' On the contrary, I have shown how far the evil can go, when God is absent." And Maurice Rostand smiles at me, a sad smile, beneath the shade of his exuberant locks.

V
INDEPENDENTS

COLETTE

COLETTE

The scent of narcissus, with its suggestion of honey and springtime, evokes for me the image of Colette. Her pensive face, thin and feline, her wildly-flying cloud of reddish hair, her head supported on a muscular arm, which rests on the table. . . The snow-white petals had been thrown into a crystal glass on a small side-table. Their odour was overpowering. . .

That evening we had seen the sun sink behind the Tuileries, and night had fallen. It was an ordinary, tranquil winter's night but Paris was in darkness—the electric light had failed. A wire had broken. Such is the price of progress. People in the streets collided against each other, bemoaning their discomfort. The arcades of the Palais-Royal took on fantastic shapes in the semi-obscurity. . .

A number of young people had met together, Charensol, Jean Larnac and Payen, at Colette's, among her books and *bibelots*. In the light of an oil lamp, without a shade, Colette was at the telephone, venting her righteous wrath and insisting on her electric light being restored to her. She talked like thunder, her Burgundian accent adding terror to her words. She appealed to us as witnesses—then wanted to turn us out. The bull-dog growled, the cats had taken refuge under the sofa. And Colette's anger did not die out.

How angry she was! And how sweet-tempered a moment later!

She frightened us, only to enchant us all the more. When we had promised to take all kinds of measures and all kinds of reprisals, she calmed down. Presently she opened some old copy-books with printed leaves and read us reminiscences of her happy girlhood and some letters of her mother's. Her hands were soft, her features were serene again. I sat looking at this woman, a massive figure in her chestnut-coloured velvet jacket. Painted eyebrows and eyelashes. A long nose give regularity to her face and ends, very thin, just above her mouth. Her glance, whose charm will hold an entire audience and win its applause, is at once keen and enveloping—index to a mind sagacious and resolute. Without giving way to emotion, she goes on reading the letters. Her rapid utterance has taken on a simplicity which helps to bring home to us the mother's love and all the ingenuous and touching pre-occupations of the children clustered round her in those far-off days. . .

Colette gives to her own youth that attentive indulgent consideration which helped her more than did her father, old soldier and *littérateur* as he was, to acquire sensitiveness and courage in life.

Imperishable memories of childhood, given out

lavishly in all her books, and in which vibrates with infinite tenderness a grateful woman's heart. Earliest sensations whose imprint was never to be effaced from the mind of the little savage a-thirst for books, with her long plaits of hair blowing about in the wind. It was in that home of hers and in her school also that she learnt "the importance of the stupid little things of life." It was there that Minet-Chéri and Bel-Gazou felt the richness and the reality of emotion.

The house had its creepers and its trellis-work and terrace. . . One day Colette was to become a marvellous landscape-painter: always her tremulous soul had steeped itself in Nature; always she wanted to see animals and plants about her growing as though in the wilds. Her love of animals dates from those days—her love of those dogs and cats "which respect her dreams" and seem to understand them. She is an animal-lover without a peer.

Paul Reboux in his monograph, "Colette, or the Genius of Style," explains her devotion to animals: "Without doubt it is because she has known much of men," he says wittily. And, in truth, Colette has suffered much from men, the principal causes of her sadness. Unhappy unions, adventures, meetings of *La Vagabonde* or of Claudine; and one day she mournfully threw off her Vrilles de la Vigne. All her work—romanced autobiography—exhales a sadness kept under: "I, discouraged? Oh no, no, indeed! Life is too short!"

Psychologist of the immortal Chéri and of Mitsou, Music Hall painter, Colette, vagabond and *frondeuse*, has remained a lone woman. Greedy of sensations, living her solitary life, determined to earn her own living. It was now she began to write her masterpieces, into which she put her entire self, tremulous, voluptuous, intensely poetical; for her most beautiful jewels, as Jean Larnac has said, are "*son jardin, son cœur, sa chair.*"

She became "*la grande Colette*"—story-writer, journalist, editress, actress and playwright.

She has rehabilitated the natural woman, glorified the pangs of the heart, in opposition to intellectualism. . .

"La Maison de Claudine," "La Retraite Sentimentale," "Les Vrilles de la Vigne" and "Dialogues" are poignant books, to be read over and over again. . .

Colette has made her home in the Palais Royal, *à l'entresol.* If I raise my hand, I touch the ceiling of the long, gallery-like room which forms almost the whole of her dwelling. "Toby-chien" nestles on the carpet in front of the charcoal fire while the cats slumber, with one eye open, on the sofa. On the wall are countless drawings of birds. Flowers everywhere, roses in a vase, roses painted on the ceiling. And everywhere curios of glass—trumpets, swords, bows, paper-weights, pears, canes, ex-votos. Some antique pots. Cretonnes upon fragile, antique tables. . . Such is the modest and happy retreat in which she is writing her new novel.

Rising nimbly from her chair, she shows me one of her glass treasures. A cat follows her about. She lifts it and places it on her arm. "Sing Prrrrou! Sing!" and the cat responds. Colette talks to me of the sunlight at Saint-Tropez. Her eyes sparkle. . . . I remember how they blazed. . . The scent of the narcissus comes back to me. . .

RAYMONDE MACHARD

RAYMONDE MACHARD

A handwriting remarkable for its tall letters which slope away like poplars seen from an express train. A haughty flourish at the end. Modulations of a pure caressing voice, just a trifle precious, coming over the telephone.

The slender, delicate hand has only one ring on it. A rectangular antique ring which covers the finger with its signet—snow-white and emerald. Her face bent forward, seductive in the perfection of its oval; its profile as clear as the lines of the eyebrows, the nostrils and skilfully tinted lips, whose smile reveals the pearly gleam of beautiful teeth. Brilliantly dark eyes with long lashes. A rounded brow flanked by wings of glowingly black hair cropped short at the back of the head.

Her fur coat, thrown open, reveals the pure line of her neck. Pearl ear-rings. A bracelet of pearls. Slender, graceful legs, very high-heeled shoes of some rare leather. Smart cloak, the creation of some great courturier: "I am a Parisian. I drive my own car, I sing, I swim, I run." She has founded the Club of *Les Uns chez les Unes*. She is a coquette and wears dazzling costumes. Her novels sell over 110,000 copies each. She knows all Paris. Her photographs and autographs are displayed in shop windows. She has good reason to know her value as an author. In short, she is Raymonde Machard.

The bustle of the Quartier des Ternes, two minutes from the Bois, suits her own active bustling temperament. She frequents all *milieux*, the better to penetrate into the secrets of the human heart: "I have friends in all the worlds." She enjoys a life of incident and excitement.

Feminine grace and luxury pervade the salon, with its *vert d'eau* colour-scheme, its tapestries, its bookshelves, its writing-desk. In this flat which she shares with the writer, Alfred Machard, her husband, everything seems to palpitate with vivid life.

I arrive. Immediately I am shown the agreement with Flammarion for the novel out this very day. The first edition is to be of 60,000 copies—doubtless with author's royalties to match—and the publisher will conduct an elaborate publicity campaign. . .

"There is a sensible and practical side to me," Raymonde Machard remarks, and she tells me, too, that the racial characteristics of Ireland blend in her with the ardour she traces back to Florentine ancestors. . . When, in her very early youth, she first became conscious of poetic and artistic aspirations, her father, a sober bourgeois, decided that she should go on the stage, and, with the Théâtre Français or the Opéra Comique in his mind, he sent her to the Conservatoire. She distinguished herself there. But, after pondering over what would be necessary to enable her to become a star, he preferred to abandon the idea of the theatre.

Then she began to write stories and sketches, and tried her hand at journalism: "I am a bad journalist, because I am too *dilettante* and I always want to labour over articles which ought to be quite slight." Henry Bataille, Rosny Ainé, Paul Adam, encouraged her. Then came the War, then marriage. A first novel, "Tu Enfanteras," which came out serially in the *Mercure de France*, obtained a prize from the Academy and a subscription from the Ville de Paris which multiplied the sales. Half novel, half autobiography, it told of the birth of a child of whom she was bereft on the very day the book appeared.

"L'Œuvre de Chair," ("my first real novel," she calls it), in which she exalts the Wife, had a large sale also, and was translated into several languages. Next came "La Possession," after three years of work. "I did not wish to exploit the success of 'L'Œuvre de Chair'; I was very industrious and I made a very elaborate study which deserves the reception that was accorded to it." In it she sings the woman in love. "Eve" is to be the title of her next book, a story of a modern woman earning her own livelihood, handicapped by the covetousness of men. . .

What are the causes of Raymonde Machard's immense success?

To begin with, her preoccupation with primary aspects of life—with Love, Avarice, Voluptuousness, etc. Exceptional aspects of life do not interest her so much. Her three novels are brimful of mother-love, the love of a wife, the love of a mistress.

Secondly, assiduous, careful work, thoughtful study of the workings of the soul and of the body. There is a passionate pathos in the last scenes of "L'Œuvre de Chair" and of "La Possession." Then she combines a keen sense of the picturesque with her psychological insight into love. Her determination to qualify herself by solid knowledge obliged her in the case of her third book to be present at a Cæsarian operation, whose horrors she witnessed quite calmly. In a word, she consecrates herself entirely to feminine interests. "I believe woman to be an idealist. Her dreams, her reactions, her sufferings, are to be understood only by a woman. And in my work I choose to study only powerful feminine creatures."

Incontestable ability is at the back of the firm structure of her novels. She understands balance. "By my faith as a writer I claim that if the great public approves me, it is for a good reason."

We shall soon be applauding "La Possession." which she has adapted for the stage.

SUZANNE NORMAND

SUZANNE NORMAND

"We women. . ." Suzanne Normand is a woman. She has of set purpose mastered the entire significance of that word. She has known the bitterness and tragedy of womanhood. Her head is held erect like that of an antique statue, making profession of its humanity.

What energy breathes from this face, with its regular features, framed in chestnut hair, cut short and pulled back almost savagely. . . The chin is strong, the large grey eyes have a steady gaze. Power and reflectiveness. A look of maturity. A magnificent physique. Decision, swiftness of thought are visible in the young, virile face in which yet no single womanly charm is missing. The authoritative bearing, the pride justified by years of struggle. . . The misery endured did not bend this body, did not abase this brow.

A woman of action, a journalist, but above all a novelist, Suzanne Normand is one of the most charming specimens of the woman of to-day— of the women who were twenty-one at the time of the Armistice. It looked as if the peace would terminate an era of privations and heroic sufferings, but it was a new era of the same kind that ensued for the girls who had no dowry, whose solicitude had sent them to work in the hospitals and munitions factories. They saw a generation of men returning from the front. They refused the sordidness of "marriage at any price" and defended their independence.

Suzanne Normand is from Savoy and of a University family, Her father, a professor, was the author of several books. Her mother also had literary gifts. When the War was over, having made up her mind to work, she left her family and settled down in Paris. In 1918 she sent in her first novel, "Tu aimeras dans la Douleur," to a competition and won a Prix de l'Aide. Then she gave herself up to journalism, joining the staff of a daily in order to go through the mill thoroughly. For several years she kept on at this work on a pitiful salary. "I experienced many discomforts," she says. "I think of those years as years of slavery. Around me I saw intelligent women wearing themselves out from morning till night for a pittance. . ."

By dint of tenacity her lot improved. She became private secretary to an author. Suddenly, two years ago, a new novel of her own, "Cinq Femmes sur une Galère," won success and fame for her. A cry poignant to assail the deaf, slashing at the egoists, describing with extreme frankness modern feminine life. She depicts the struggle of these exceptional women working side by side with men. Certain critics tried to crush the book. . .

"It was really a galley-slave existence," she

declares. "It enabled me to consider the eternal verities at my own expense." Her talk is friendly and she has had excellent friends, both men and women, and has not had to endure feminine jealousy: Men? Mostly gross, brutal, ignorant of feminine finesse. And the unhappiness of women lies in this, that they are made for. "They need masculine support. I totally disapprove of free love. It spells nothing but disaster."

Women without men? Well, they cannot keep going. They have the courage but not the means. "Happiness, for a woman, is to be loved more than she loves. Short of that, misery."

"La Maison de Laideur et de Lésine" followed later, a book marked by appalling bitterness. . .

Her little flat is in a house at Saint-Mande. A landscape by Goya, a picture of a child by Greuze, a sepia sketch by Lebrun, a water-colour by Hébert. A drawing of a sad-faced woman by Ricart. A seascape by Boudin. Specimens of the work of Thornley, Whistler, Bourguignon. A rustic box, a peasant's *fromager*, shawls, flowers, a Louis XIIIth cabinet. Her own portrait by Marguerye, a pen-drawing tinted. . .

A room with a welcome, a cordial to both eye and heart. . . Suzanne Normand is emancipated, intellectually active, with a tender heart and noble sentiments. Love is an unavoidable mischance, yet still to be desired. . .

TITAYNA

TITAYNA

She is an inhabitant of "Metropolis."

On the outskirts of Paris there now stands some tremendous blocks of buildings, almost skyscrapers. Their vast façade is pierced by windows innumerable. There are inner courtyards, artificial little gardens, caretakers' lodges, a central telephone-hall. The staircases are all numbered. . .

"Distances nowadays have no meaning apart from time. And we live so fast that time is going up in value." Titayna runs her own car and her own aeroplane, she rides, she is an intrepid swimmer, a bold explorer, a woman of education. She has hob-nobbed with cannibals and has wandered over all the seas. . . She is young and pretty. She began by living through nine years of austerity in a Dominican convent.

Appointed a *dame d'honneur* in 1923 to a Princess of the Imperial House of Japan, she travelled in Europe with the latter, and both of them were seriously injured in an accident in which the Japanese Prince lost his life. After three months in a hospital she set out in an aeroplane to visit Czecho-Slovakia, Austria, Hungary, Dalmatia and Montenegro. A lecture tour followed in Roumania, and then one in Corsica, where she came across Romanetti. Next she went off by air to Angora. The aeroplane fell into the Black Sea, but both the pilot and she got safely to land and after a journey of five days over the desert reached Constantinople. Spain, Morocco, the Riff, Egypt, Italy. Next an attempt with Thoret to alight on Mont Blanc—the machine crashed down in the Jura. She embarked on a tramp steamer and went to the Antilles, Panama, Tahiti. She has been one of the crew of a sailing vessel, calling first at the islands of Sous le Vent and the Marquesas, then going on to New Caledonia, Australia, Japan, China, Cambodia. . . Expeditions as a correspondent for great foreign newspapers, etc., etc. A vagrant cosmopolitan, she confesses to restlessness, to a love of travel for its own sake. This it is that has turned her into a journalist like Paul Morand and many others whose wanderings have given new life to our literature. "Mor Tour du Monde" is Titayna, the seeker, cheating her natural melancholy by using the world as a kaleidoscope.

Her alert mind notes the diversity of the various civilizations, primitive and otherwise, the diversity of prejudices and points of view—the whole fantasia of our epoch, of which she is typical, as she is of our literature. . . Fittingly enough, she has just taken over the editorship of *Jazz*, an excellent and very modern review dealing with literary and international topics.

She dresses like a man. . .

Chrysanthemums; a panel of a Breton bed;

some pictures. A portrait of herself by Faoryi: "People think I am a Hindoo. I am a Parisienne!"

A book by Delteil, with risky illustrations; sketches of women by Mariette Lydis. . . A comfortable room, soft carpets; souvenirs from all corners of the world—a crab from the cocoatrees of Oceania, a wooden bowl from the Marquesas, birds made out of horn from Madagascar, the jaw of a sacred pig of the New Hebrides, a weird dagger, a fan signed by members of the Imperial family of Japan, an ikon, the horns of a stag shot in New Caledonia. . .

She talks to me of her travels and experiences, tells stories of her narrow escapes, touches on politics, psychology, art. Intellectuality, pride, coquetry and romance abound in her life. "*Reportages décevants*" she calls her books "Voyage autour de mon Amant" and "Voyage autour de ma Maitresse" . . .

To-morrow she is off to Persia. She is a solitary woman, leading a solitary life. Always on the move. A saying of hers: "It is a sad reflection that everything you learn takes you one step further into isolation."

VI
WAYFARERS

MAURICE DEKOBRA

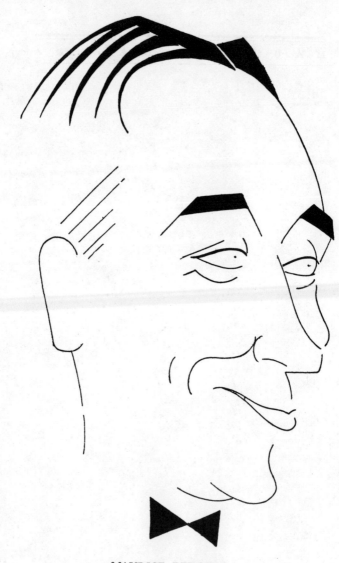

MAURICE DEKOBRA

From the submarine we stepped into the yacht. After the close quarters of the cabin containing the periscope, the manometer, and other contrivances, we found ourselves in a luxurious cabin, the glazed roof of which admitted a softly diffused sunlight. The walls and doors painted white, mahogany furniture, bronze fittings. Through the port-holes there came in a breeze from the ocean—one could picture the endless expanse of waves. Life-belts handy, a chart of Europe. The engines must have stopped working for there was no noise. Maurice Dekobra, all smiles (especially his lower lip and chin), his hair parted in the middle, elegantly garbed, elastic in his bearing, courteous but free and easy, leaving the only seat for me, somehow accommodated his supple limbs on the cabin bed. Then into the Pullman car, in which two Pullman chairs accommodated us. . . After the sea, the railway. . .

"I am forty-three," Maurice Dekobra told me. "While I was quite a young boy I ran away from my parents to camp out all alone in the mountains and become Robinson Crusoe. At seventeen I became a journalist at Rouen and was sent off to Germany, Scandinavia and Russia. At twenty I gave lectures in Berlin. Since then I have travelled unceasingly. This very evening I am off to Poland to lecture. In the War I served with an Indian regiment as liaison officer, was in touch with the English and Americans. . . In 1910 I had been through an electoral campaign. I know America through and through. Europe also, and Asia Minor. I speak English, German, Italian, Russian and Hindustani. . ."

Why was not the train moving? Where were we? I pushed aside the sliding window. Behold the Trocadero and the Tour Eiffel! . . . We had not left Paris nor the Rue Freycinet. . .

Maurice Dekobra, as you will have gathered, has turned his flat into a submarine, a yacht and a Pullman. The submarine is a bar. The binnacle presents the cocktails; from the periscope come the roasted almonds, the olives and the "chips." The yacht is his bedroom; the gangway a library; the port-holes overhang the Musée Galliera; his bed is operated by some kind of mechanism that causes it to swing—without this he cannot sleep. On the chart of Europe small flags on pins follow the movements of the heroes of his books.

A writer of humorous stories before he became the cosmopolitan novelist he now is, his first books were "Les Mémoires de Rat de Cave," "Prince ou Pitre," "Au Pays du Fox-Trot," "Grain d'Cachou," all noteworthy for their verve and volubility. From that time also comes the philosophical fantasy, "Hamydal le Philosophe," recently reprinted. These early books of his, little known to the general public, have more literary talent than his late ones.

"Paul Bourget's epoch is over. There are no longer any literary frontiers, the literature of the provinces is done with, everything has been said. But what themes remain! America alone is inexhaustible."

When he began writing his cosmopolitan books he became the most widely read of all post-war novelists. "Mon Coeur au Ralenti" and "La Madone des Sleepings" in 1924 had fabulous sales. "La Gondole aux Chimères," "Flammes de Velours," "Sérénade au Bourreau" added to his celebrity. His novels have been translated into twenty-three languages. They are written easily in a captivating modern style. . .

"The modern novelist who would document his period must not stop short at psychology. He should live amongst the people he is studying." Dekobra's own life is consistent with his theory.

"When away from France I live among foreigners, adapting myself to their mentality, adopting their ways, speaking their language." His life is a life of sky-scrapers, palace hotels, watering places, ocean liners and Jazz. "When I am writing a novel, I think of the different nationalities of my readers." An ingenious sprinkling of quotations, technical expressions, allusions to localities. Illicit love-affairs, bringing in police courts and politics. "Vamps," elopements, kidnappings, not without touches of the French poetry and chivalry, which foreigners so delight in. But he forgets to choose French heroines.

"Is cosmopolitanism a fashion?"

"No, but a contagion, and an international state of mind at once political, industrial and financial—one which keeps on growing. Its service to the nations is undeniable for it helps them to avoid war and to get to know each other better."

A porcelain parrot supports a lamp which throws its light on the "Toute la Terre" series which Dekobra edits. A photograph of Josephine Baker. A licentious caricature. On the mantelpiece a plaster bust of Hoche. Near it a scent-bottle with a label on it: "Eau de Nil"—a mascot, he explains. Reproductions of Michael Angelo and the Italian Schools. Model of a Hindoo temple. Flowers. An electric radiator. . . It is in this room that Maurice Dekobra writes, sitting between a Babenké fetish, an Egyptian scarabaeus and a Kakris dagger.

JOSEPH KESSEL

JOSEPH KESSEL

I caught the author of "Captifs" on his return from Syria, and just a few minutes before his departure for Switzerland. He fairly staggered me.

A huge monster of a fellow, with fists that could fell an ox.

A great disordered tuft of brown hair above his forehead, which is low; a flattened nose, thick lips, square jaw. The complexion of an Asiatic, lit up by dark eyes, the cornea of which is as gleamingly white as his teeth. The mask of a fighter but with a gentle, placid expression which astonishes. Nothing suggestive of the giant about his voice, which is tranquil, agreeable and marked by nonchalance and simplicity. A frank smile does much to mitigate his barbaric appearance.

Joseph Kessel is of Russian origin. He spent his childhood in the Caucasus and in the Argentine and travelled widely after that, becoming a student of acting later in Paris at the Conservatoire. He made his *début* in tragedy at the Odéon, and appeared later at the Renaissance. After the Armistice, he wrote novels. He was famous at twenty-eight. In his short stories you see the poet in him and the spectator of Russian miseries; in his novels it is the aviator you meet, and the student of the sufferings of the world in general.

"I, a man of letters? No, indeed. There is no career so hurtful to the mind. If I write, it is just to take stock of my own impressions, to analyse what I see and make a record of it. When I start on a book, I finish it as quickly as possible, then forget all about it for six months or a year. I put it away in a drawer. I am never keen to see it printed, especially as I am never satisfied with what I have written. By the time I am thirty, I shall probably have nothing more to write. I write because I want to live—I don't live to write."

An exciting existence, his. Flights hither and thither—New York, San Francisco, Honolulu, Shanghai, Colombo. Wherever political disturbances are to the fore, he appears upon the scene. . .

He writes a classic style. The Academy has bestowed on him its Grand Prix de Littérature. . . The *Revue des Deux Mondes* has opened its doors to him. . . But the air is his element. Up in his aeroplane he can breathe. . .

Nothing could be sadder than the melancholy of this heroic figure that comes to life only amidst the dangers of air and of battle. In him is the soul of the Slav, the exile, the drama of the exceptional nature that appears scarcely at all in his books.

PAUL MORAND

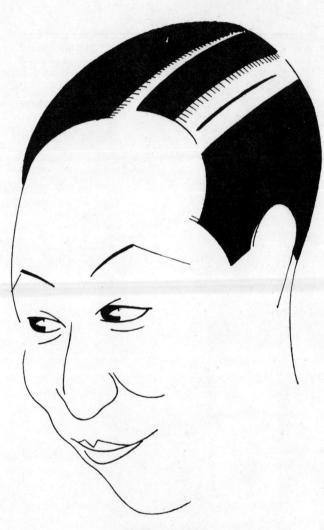

PAUL MORAND

Paul Morand is the literary vogue. His name coins money. The titles of his books are borrowed for smart teashops and the books themselves are to be found in every boudoir. Society women, reporters, organizers of literary gatherings, idealistic ladies arranging dinner-parties, compete for his presence. All the *littérateurs*, and especially the literary pontiffs, pay court to this most outstanding representative of the Quai d'Orsay school of novelists.

Impatient to meet him, I waited for the steamer that was bringing him back to Europe. After much manœuvring I had the honour of being received in his sumptuous Asiatic mansion on the Champs de Mers. The author of "Ouvert la nuit" had just left his bathroom, and he allowed me to interview him while he dressed.

Innumerable photographs have familiarized the whole world with this Japanese face, tense, muscular, with inscrutable eyes: the face of an athlete, its shape almost the Oriental oval, with black hair gleaming like lacquer. His well-knit, supple frame is carried with a deliberately Anglicized simplicity. He is as polite as a diplomat, and radiates an atmosphere of youth, sports, swimming, shower-baths, health.

His eye is like a movie-camera: he sees life in shining pictures and seeks these all over the world, which he likes to cover at a great pace, driving his own car, "the swiftest in France." He is not much of a talker, inclined to be ironical, and though his hand-writing is as brutal as might be the blows of his fist, he is entirely self-controlled. Who in following the adventures of Renaud in his "Bouddha Vivant" will not have identified him with this elegant Parisianism disgusted with Europe and seeking adventures in strange places?

Dressed in a sky-blue shirt, striped trousers and black silk slippers, Paul Morand sat upon a divan draped with Indian silk, surrounded by barbaric luxury: carved woodwork, sleeping Buddhas, massive statuary, furniture from the East and from England. Splendours of the kind a discriminating Nabob might be expected to collect.

Until last year he was in the French diplomatic service. He spent his youth in Russia, where he was born, at Oxford and Munich and Edinburgh. An attaché, now in London, now in Rome, now in Madrid. . . . His life unrolls itself like the reel of a film. He is of those who have joined "the new dance, travel," and cannot stay in one place.

In "Lampes à Arc" he showed himself one of the most brilliant chroniclers of our post-War existence with its Jazz and cocktails and shattered nerves. . . But what a change from that to "Bouddha Vivant"!

To-day he is a little ashamed of having written

"L'Europe Galante," for he wishes to be considered a serious writer. And "Rien que la Terre" is philosophical in tendency. "Bouddha Vivant" deals with the East against the West, and suggests that he might be on his way to becoming an academic. But he is intelligent and did not take long to realise that he was on the wrong road. A splendid subject offered: the Negro. "Magie Noire" reflects the accumulated complexities of the modern outlook.

Paul Morand is, *par excellence*, the French traveller of our century. He writes his books in his country house at Triannel, in Normandy. You may see him there, clad in a many-hued sweater, English breeches and thick stockings, in the company of his Alaskan sledge-dog.

I left him strapping his cabin trunk packed full of treasures: an all-steel thermos flask, a cooking outfit as neat and complex as a jig-saw puzzle, and some dresses of a gorgeous red bought in Paris for far-off friends, favourites of negro kings. . . And I remembered that horrible saying of his in "Voyage" about wishing his skin to be made into a travelling-bag when he is dead: "*Je voudrais qu'après ma mort, on fît de ma peau une valise!*"

PIERRE MAC ORLAN

PIERRE MAC ORLAN

I shall always think of this strange little man with the Scottish pseudonym as I saw him at the doorway of his house, dressed in knickerbockers and black-and-white slippers, and a pullover whose orange stripes matched his socks, watching us drive off just as he had watched our arrival: expressionlessly. With absent eyes, deep-set in a head that is round and flattened like a bird's and sports a small, wilful beak, he contemplated the snorting car, waiting to turn away the moment we had rounded the corner. We had covered at top-speed that blowy autumn morning the hundred kilometres between Paris and the peaceful hamlet with its red houses and apple orchards, so well known to Carco and Dorgelès.

A country gentleman living at his ease with his dogs and his gun, his fishing-rod, his rabbit-hutches. . . Such is this novelist of Parisian and cosmopolitan life, interpreter of modernity. "*Je ne vis jamais à la campagne,*" he declares! Yet La Brie is not without its attractions. In front of his house, the meadows slope down towards the Morin, willows droop beneath the poplars standing out against the sky-line. Hare-patties have a pleasant savour. There is no railway station. Pierre Mac Orlan seizes his hunting horn and at the risk of bursting a blood-vessel sounds his horn when the boar is sighted.

There is a rustic look about everything in the